Beneath the Surface

Libby Trickett OAM is an ambassador for Beyond Blue. A portion of author royalties from this book will be donated to assist Beyond Blue to continue supporting Australians suffering with mental illness.

LIBBY TRICKETT

WITH SIMONE UBALDI

Beneath the Surface

ALLEN&UNWIN

SYDNEY·MELBOURNE·AUCKLAND·LONDON

Allen & Unwin
83 Alexander Street
Crows Nest NSW 2065
Australia
Phone: (61 2) 8425 0100
Email: info@allenandunwin.com
Web: www.allenandunwin.com

A catalogue record for this
book is available from the
National Library of Australia

ISBN 978 1 76063 282 3

Set in 12/18 pt Sabon by Midland Typesetters, Australia
Printed and bound in Australia by Griffin Press, part of Ovato

10 9 8 7 6 5 4 3 2 1

The paper in this book is FSC® certified.
FSC® promotes environmentally responsible,
socially beneficial and economically viable
management of the world's forests.

To those who have known darkness.
You are not alone, there will be light again.
This is for you.

Chapter One

2012

'The wound is the place where the light enters you.'

—Rumi

There are no waiting times for elite athletes. When the pain in my wrist doesn't lift, I go to see one of the leading sports doctors in Brisbane; he sends me for an MRI and refers me to a specialist, and I get in straightaway. I go to Dr Phillip Duke in his private rooms at St Andrew's Hospital, where the walls are lined with autographed rugby jerseys and sporting memorabilia. He treats the Wallabies and the Queensland Reds, so he knows a sporting injury when he sees one. And he knows exactly what he's looking at when he sees my scans. 'You've had a catastrophic injury to your wrist,' he says. 'It's a full tear of the scapholunate, and it could very easily mean the end of your swimming career.'

This is confronting—of course it is. The word 'cata-strophic' is confronting. But the end of my swimming career? How is that even possible? I haven't been in a car accident or had a severe fall. I'm not a footballer—I don't get smashed around on the field every week. I was doing weights at the gym one day and felt a twang in my wrist. And now we're talking about the end?

In twenty years of competitive swimming, including three Olympic Games, I have never had a single injury. Okay, so I'm injured now, but that doesn't mean it's over. I feel like I only just found my groove again. I came out of retirement, I swam at the London Games. I've only just rediscovered my passion for swimming, that real love of the water. So it can't be over now—I won't let it be. *No worries*, I think to myself. *I'll come back from this.* But the word 'catastrophic' keeps bouncing around in my head.

I want to go to my fourth Olympics so badly I can taste it. After a while, your career is not about any single gold medal, it's about longevity. It's about how long you can perform at that level. The pack starts to fall away, and you find yourself in a rarer and rarer crowd, the elite of the elite. And you get a rush from chasing that kind of distinction. I'm swimming for my legacy. This goal has become weird and obscure, but it's still a goal, something out in front of me that I can strive for, that drives me forward. It's something that I can channel all of my competitive spirit into, that restless energy that has always been inside me. Three Olympics is impressive, but four is legendary. If I swim at four Olympic Games, history will remember me. I don't mean to sound egotistical—I just want people to think of me fondly, the way I think about the great swimmers who came before me.

Anyway, I'm not there yet. I haven't achieved enough. There are so many people who have won more medals than me, and at fewer Olympics. There are people who have swum at more Games, and there are people with more world records. I'm never going to beat everyone, but I'm not done trying. At the very least, I have to make it to the World Championships in Barcelona next year, in 2013. It will be the tenth anniversary of the first time I qualified for the World Championship team, when I went to Barcelona in 2003. Ten years swimming at an elite level, bookended in one of my favourite cities in the whole world—what a perfect moment. I can't even contemplate not making it.

It was a maybe. Maybe my career will be over, maybe it won't. Phillip refers me on to a wrist specialist, Dr Mark Ross, who recommends a full wrist reconstruction. I've never heard of a wrist reconstruction; it turns out they are quite rare, and as a result maybe ten or fifteen years behind knee and shoulder reconstructions in how sophisticated they are. Mark and a fellow doctor have pioneered a new procedure, which only twenty or so people have had before me. It involves drilling through five bones in the wrist and threading a piece of ligament through the hole, then anchoring it on the far side of the wrist. They've seen some great success in the short term, but they don't have any long-term results. That makes no difference to me. This is my only hope—what choice do I have? Mark thinks it'll take around three months for me to rehab and get back into training—assuming the procedure works.

The surgery is scheduled for December 2012, and I'm in the pool right up until the day I have to go into hospital. I'm doing a lot of kick work, keeping my legs strong while my wrist is out of action. Three months is fine, I think. Barcelona is not going to happen, but I can have three months out and still get back in form and on track for the Rio Olympics in 2016. I'll scale everything back, do what I can, keep my diet up, keep my cardio up, and I'll be good. So many people have come back from severe injuries, I tell myself. Petria Thomas came back from three shoulder reconstructions—three! Eamon Sullivan had eight hip surgeries, countless cortisone injections, a broken foot. He had severe shoulder issues and back issues, but he came back, so I will too. That's all there is to it. I am a doggedly optimistic person—pig-headed, some might say. But that attitude has always served me well—it helped me become a champion—so why should I behave any differently now?

The surgery is a success, but it's incredibly painful. I've never had any trouble sleeping before but I find that if I roll the wrong way in bed or Luke, my husband, knocks me in his sleep, I wake up with my wrist throbbing and break into tears. I'm on strong pain medication but it doesn't touch the sides, especially in the first few days. The ache is constant. I'm used to pain, to pushing through aching muscles and tiredness in the pool, but this takes me by surprise. The swelling is intense, too. I feel really off-balance, and training in the pool is out of the question. I try to get back onto the exercise bike, to keep my metabolism up, and I do whatever I can at the gym that isn't weight-bearing, but it's not much. My body really needs a timeout, but my athlete's brain kicks in. Okay, I can't swim—but I can run. I can work on my core, maintain my fitness. I can improve the parts of my repertoire that don't usually get focused attention, and make them even stronger. I can maintain my momentum.

The weird thing about this is that it has all happened so fast. I trained for two weeks after hurting my wrist, before I realised it was serious. I booked in with the physio and they told me I had tight forearms, but massage didn't help. Two weeks after that I was in surgery, and now I'm here. My life has taken a very sharp turn, and my head is still spinning. I make an appointment with my sports psychologist, Georgia Ridler, to help me stay positive. Georgia has a lot of experience working with athletes, though a lot of it is performance-based. She helps with mental preparedness on the day of a race, which is a specific component of training. But if athletes are struggling with self-esteem or other mental-health issues, Georgia is a good person to see. She knows how we think.

Georgia is warm, and I find her really easy to talk to. I make an appointment with her not long after the surgery not because I feel sad or angry, but because I know that seeing a psychologist is a smart thing to do. It's part of a high-performance mindset, part of my training, to use all the available resources to keep me on track.

Georgia helps me develop a strategy to get through this period by helping me focus on what I can control. Acceptance is key. I can't control the fact that I have the injury, and I can't control how long it's going to take me to recover, but I can control my diet, I can control my attitude, and there is so much that I can do, that I can focus on. Once the stitches are out and the wound has healed, I can get back in the water and do some kicking exercises. That's what I can control. That's what we focus on. That's how, step by step, I'll get back in the water.

I don't know how I got from there to here. There's no one moment when everything unravels, just an accumulation of time. It's a slow winding down, like the air leaking out of a balloon. I start training less and less as time goes by. In the first three months, I am in rehabilitation, healing the wound. In the month or so that follows, I get in the pool and do what little I can. I do my kick sets, try to strengthen my legs, step through the process. I am waiting for the pain in my wrist to ease so that I can step up my training and restart my weight-bearing routine in the gym. But as another month passes, and drifts into two, the pain doesn't improve—or it doesn't improve enough. At first I'm patient, but time starts weighing on me. Every month of peak training I lose makes it less likely that I'll be able to claw my way back.

I spent a year out of the pool in 2009, when for a brief and depressing moment I thought I was done with swimming. I gained 10 kilograms in those twelve months and lost my edge completely. It was such a grind to get back in shape, because I was so far off my peak. And that was three years ago. I'm now 28 and keenly aware that, in the swimming world, I'm a geriatric. It's not impossible for me to be the best, but it's already an uphill battle, and that's without this recovery period dragging on and on. I'm starting to doubt that, when I do get back, I'll be able to swim at the level I want to. My goals are getting hazier, because they're further and further out of reach.

But what am I supposed to do, if not this? I have no idea who I am if I'm not a swimmer; my brief flirtation with retirement in 2009 really drove that point home. I have no other skills, no training, no plan B. And I don't want to do anything else. I wish I could compete forever.

Luke is incredibly supportive. We've been through rough patches before, and we both know that communication is key, so he keeps checking in to see how I'm doing. But there's no pressure, no expectations—he just wants me to do what's right for me, and I'm incredibly grateful for that. But as the doubt creeps in, I start wondering how we're going to get by. I've been the primary breadwinner throughout our relationship, at first because my career was going well and then because Luke had a new business, and always paid himself last. I'm nervous about how we'll manage if I'm not swimming. It's uncharted water.

These thoughts sneak in quietly and begin taking up space in my brain. It's a gentle creep, month after month, dulling my competitive edge. I think it's a form of kindness, really. Like my subconscious mind knows that I can't deal with what is coming, so it loosens the cap just a little bit and lets the air leak ever so slowly out of my dreams. I so desperately want to keep swimming. I don't want the last year to have been a waste—the hours I've spent in the pool, the weight training, sacrifices. My body and my heart have accepted that I have to move on, but my mind is slow to catch up. I know that this is a process I have to go through. I think the actual injury was necessary, because I would never have retired of my own volition. And that's what I have to do: I have to retire. And this time I will not go back.

When I announced my first retirement from swimming in 2009, I just wanted to get it over with, but my manager at the time counselled me to wait until I knew what I was going to do next. 'You're not retiring from something, you're retiring to something,' he told me. 'It's a much better look.'

I've got nothing to retire to this time. I have to tell people that I'm retiring from swimming and I'm drifting off into oblivion, with no further plans. The path ahead is totally dark—that's the honest truth. But I have a new manager, and she's also of the opinion that I should retire with a forward schedule, and failing that I should just make one up. 'Go out on a positive note and people will remember you in a positive way,' she says. She's wangled some early meetings about a reality TV show proposal that I might be involved with, and even though it's a bit premature we agree that this is what I'll mention when people ask me what's next. Apparently, 'I have no idea and I'm terrified' is not an acceptable answer.

I'm scheduled to appear on *The Project* in July 2013, seven months after the operation. It's time. Part of me wonders if I should even bother making a formal announcement, but it seems to be the done thing and it's better for my career. I'm thinking about this while sitting in hair and make-up at the Channel 10 studio in Melbourne. *What career, seriously? My career is behind me.* But the hope is that opportunities will present themselves if people know I'm not busy in the pool. If the reality TV show actually gets off the ground, I'll be a media personality, I suppose, but I wish I didn't have to mention it in the same breath as the end of my Olympic dreams. One of these things means the whole world to me, and the other means nothing at all.

There's a huge spread of food and drink laid out in the green room, but I don't touch it. I'm nervous. I've been in front of the camera so many times that it doesn't usually bother me, but this time is different because my life is about to change. Once the words are out of my mouth, it's done and I can't take them back. Once I say it on live television, it's real. I've been dreading this moment ever since I made the decision, and part of me wants to turn around and run. Another part of me is calm. Later, when I'm alone in the hotel room, thinking it all through, I will remember everything I have achieved over the last ten years and I will feel proud. *You did a great job, Libby, you really did.* But right now there are knots in my stomach.

A production assistant comes to collect me, and we walk into the studio where *The Project* is filming. I marvel once again at how small everything looks in real life—the studio itself, the desk, the audience. But the lights are startlingly bright, and I can feel the adrenaline building as I take my seat and say hello to the hosts, who are shuffling their papers and getting ready to come back from the commercial break. Then the red light on the camera flicks on and everyone is smiling at me; all kind people. And I smile back and tell them that my swimming career is over.

1992

'The secret of getting ahead is getting started.'

—Mark Twain

One of my earliest memories of swimming was at a carnival in Charters Towers, up in North Queensland, where we lived when I was a kid. I had broken my wrist a week earlier and I insisted on having a waterproof cast. It was designed to let me have showers or have a bath while I was healing, but in my mind it was all about swimming. I just wanted to get back in the pool.

There weren't many opportunities to compete in that part of the world, so my family travelled quite a bit to attend carnivals like the one in Charters Towers. My brother and sisters were going to swim but I wasn't registered. Mum had decided, pretty reasonably, that a little girl with a broken wrist probably couldn't swim in a race. I disagreed. I badgered her until she finally gave in, signing me up for the 50-metre freestyle the day before the competition.

Poor Mum spent the morning fending off questions about why her daughter was registered to swim when she was wearing a cast, but they didn't understand how determined I was, how single-minded, even as a kid. There was no stopping me. 'When can I swim?' I'd whine. 'When can I swim, Mum? Why won't you let me? Is it my turn yet? I want to get in the water!'

She always said I was a bit of a nightmare until it was my time to race. I would fidget and get into mischief, running wild around the pool while she was trying to wrangle four kids. But afterwards, when I'd finished my race, I was a perfect angel, placid as a doll—maybe the only time I've been placid in my life. I was a headstrong little thing, extremely stubborn, and my mum, Marilyn, was the gentlest, most accommodating person imaginable. She always bent over backwards for her children, but at Charters Towers she was probably just picking her battles. I don't know if jumping into the water was the best idea—I don't know if the waterproof cast was really designed for a chlorinated pool—but I wasn't going to have it any other way.

I won my heat that day, broken wrist and all. I was so proud of myself—I knew I'd done really well against the odds. After I swam, I ate hot chips and red frogs. I remember thinking it had been the best day ever.

*

When it came to sport, I was very good at following instructions. I was good at gymnastics when I was little. I had tennis lessons too, and would wait patiently in line for my turn to have a swing at the ball that the instructor popped gently over the net, and I would scurry around afterwards collecting the stray balls before jumping back in the queue. I loved being active and I was very focused, at least when I was outdoors. School was very different—I was never really comfortable—but when I was running or jumping or swimming, I was like an arrow heading straight for the target. I was very compliant when I knew I was going to get a turn. If I didn't get to play, or didn't know when I was going to play, I was probably pretty dreadful. My nerves were constantly tingling, ready to fire, a wriggling sack of beans.

I was the baby of the family, which probably didn't help. I had two older sisters, Justine and Victoria, and an older brother, Stewart, who was closest to me in age but still almost four years older. We lived in Townsville, where I was born, but we would often visit the cane farm up north where my mother grew up, where we'd spend the weekend riding quad bikes and climbing trees, exploring cane fields and swimming in the river. At home in Townsville, we had a backyard pool, which was crucial in that baking tropical climate. We loved the heat, loved the outdoors and spent endless hours in the water. There was something magical about diving out of the muggy air and into the crisp, cool water of a swimming pool. That's where my love of swimming started.

Our whole social world seemed to be built around water, whether it was swimming at home or going to the beach, or hanging out along The Strand in Towns-ville, which was down by the water. We learned to swim very young, probably for safety as much as anything else; I wasn't more than a year old when I started. My siblings were all doing their lessons and I was just along for the ride, a mini paddler in the baby pool who was quickly diving hell-for-leather into the deep end. Most Australian kids learn to swim in summer, but it felt like summer all year round in Townsville. I had a swimming lesson every week, and I joined my first swimming club when I was four. From then on, there were club meets every Friday night, with a sausage sizzle and ice-cream when the racing was done. It was just what my family did, for as long as I could remember.

My first-ever race was a 25-metre breaststroke. I always hated breaststroke, but boy did I love competing. I just fell in love with it, even as a four-year-old. *Cool, I can see how fast I go!* I thought. What could be more exciting than being fast? Usually parents would jump in the water to help the very little kids through the race, and my dad was next to me trying to help keep me afloat, but I wasn't having it—I was annoyed that he was getting in the way. The four-year-old age group wasn't exactly teeming with competitors, but I wasn't thinking about the other kids in the pool. From the very beginning, I just wanted to be a rocket, to speed through the water, and I loved, loved, loved how it felt to kick as hard as I could and churn my arms until I touched the wall. I remember that feeling so well—that absolute thrill. I'd be chasing it for the rest of my life.

Oddly, that first race is one of the only memories I have of my father. He was a successful ophthalmologist, and he worked long hours. In fact, he prided himself on being a workaholic. He may also have travelled for work—I don't actually know—but for various reasons he wasn't much of a presence in my life.

It was my second swimming coach, Luc Senent, who recognised that I had talent in the pool. My family had moved from the Aitkenvale Swimming Club at Kokoda pool to the Townsville Tourists at the Tobruk pool on The Strand, by which time I had already been competing for a few years. Luc wasn't an elite-level coach but he was exactly what I needed at the time. At seven or eight years old, I was a headstrong little fish, and I was absolutely devoted to racing, and Luc was excellent at helping me develop my skills while keeping everything fun. We had a special ritual at training where both of us would inflate our bellies with air and stick them out as far as they could go—I was very proud of my bulbous tummy. Everything about training and swimming carnivals was fun back then, although I had started a journey that would ultimately become very significant for me.

Every step was a small one. At first I was racing just to reach the end of the pool, then to win a ribbon or a trophy from my club, and then I was racing to qualify as a junior competitor in the State Championships—I just needed to get a fast enough time.

As an eight-year-old in 1994, I was swimming in the Under-10s category, so some of the kids were a year or two older than me, though not necessarily much faster. I qualified for the 100-metre butterfly final at States for the first time that year, which was very cool. I was crazy nervous. I always needed Mum's help to get my swimming cap on, and this time I asked her to put my goggles on for me too, to make sure they were perfect. From the moment I left the grandstand until I was on the starting block I was wearing my goggles, and so by the time I got to the block they were completely fogged over. I couldn't see a thing. Still, I did a massive personal best time to qualify for the finals. I finished dead last in the final, and was very disappointed, but overall it felt like a win. I was determined to come back and do better next time.

We went to the State Championships in Brisbane every year after that, at what used to be called Chandler and is now the Brisbane Aquatic Centre. They were held in January, during the school holidays, and it was always a huge event for our family. We'd make the long drive down from Townsville and stay at the Dockside apartments, near Kangaroo Point—small-town kids in the big city for the biggest swimming event of my year. We often drove a couple of hours to attend swimming carnivals, but this was something else altogether: fifteen hours down the Bruce Highway for a couple of days of competition. I don't know how Mum did it! I think she enjoyed it because she knew it made us happy.

For me it was always a joyful time. I remember the feeling so clearly—an eager, hungry kind of happiness. I *loved* to compete. Winning a medal or coming first was great, but that wasn't what drove me. I didn't want to be better than other people; I was just very focused on doing better than I had before. I wanted to improve on my best time, every time. If that meant I won a medal, great—but the medal wasn't the point. I just wanted to go faster.

When I was ten years old, I moved with Mum and my siblings to Brisbane. My father didn't come with us; I was told he would be joining us at some point, though the timing was always vague. Later in 1995 I went to Perth to compete in the Western Australian Pacific School Games, and we stayed with my sister Justine, who was living there at the time. Mum told us after the meet that she and Dad were getting a divorce. I remember sitting in a hot tub with my sister Victoria, trying to figure out what it meant. I didn't know what a divorce was or how it would affect me. In fact, my father was already such a ghost that it hardly made a difference.

I could sense the grief and stress in my mother, but I was shielded from the truth for many years. I heard the late-night phone calls and heated conversations, but I was well into my teens before anyone told me about my father's affair. Perhaps he thought leaving his wife meant leaving his children behind as well, but however rarely we had seen him before, it was nothing compared to the years after the divorce. My father did move down to Brisbane eventually, with his new wife and his new child, but he made no attempt to see the rest of his kids with any consistency. Two or three times a year he would pick us up and take us to the movies. He'd buy us a book or a toy and drop us home, and that would be it for several months. I felt no connection to him at all—it was like hanging out with a distant relative who lived in another country. Even though I knew he should be someone very important to me, these outings always felt forced and awkward. We weren't picking up where we left off, as there was nothing there. Whatever natural yearning I had to have a father didn't match up with what he had to offer.

We were so lucky to have Mum. She cared for us and loved us to a fault. She cleaned my room for me every week and put dinner on the table every night, and bent over backwards to give us everything she could. It's easy to think that she was trying to make up for the fact that our father wasn't around, but I think it was just her nature to be selfless. She was quietly but fiercely supportive of me; she believed in me even before I believed in myself.

In 1999, when I was fourteen, I failed to qualify for the finals at States for the first time. I didn't make a single race. And there was a very good explanation for it: I was a massive bludger. Up until that point, I had been coasting on my talent and doing to the bare minimum at training, while girls around me like Amy Townend, Sarah Bowd and Katie Canning were in the pool ten times a week. They were committed, and the results were starting to show; they were outswimming me at carnivals, and that year it finally came to a head. Not only did I not win anything, I wasn't even a contender. All the thrill of competition suddenly evaporated.

I was devastated on the ride home from Chandler. Mum couldn't stand seeing me so upset, so she consoled me in the best way she knew. 'Don't worry about it,' she said. 'You tried your best. You don't have to swim next year. Let's just forget about it.'

I thought about this for a while, trying to figure out how I felt about her proposal. For me, the joy in swimming came from competing—but if I wasn't competitive, what was the point? I wasn't happy being average. But the thought of losing swimming made me feel incredibly uneasy. Between the divorce and our move to Brisbane, there had been some big shifts in my life. I had also just hit puberty, and I had started to discover boys, so in addition to being a people pleaser in general, I was suddenly struck by an urgent need to feel validated by the opposite sex. Everything was changing, but I had always been a swimmer, and it felt like the last solid thing I could hold on to, the last thing that was comfortable and familiar. I didn't want to give that up.

I also didn't want to lose—which posed a real problem. Ultimately, I decided that if I wanted to stick with swimming, then I had to train a bit harder.

At that stage, I was in the pool four times a week, and I'd made a habit of taking things easy. My signature move was to say I had to go to the toilet, then spend fifteen minutes killing time under a warm shower in the change rooms. I'd skip laps, I'd sit on the edge of the pool pretending to fix my goggles for five minutes, I'd don flippers for sets that were supposed to increase my heartrate and stamina. Basically, I'd cheat whenever I got the chance.

After that disastrous State Championships meet, I was a new swimmer. I didn't skip laps, I ditched the fins, I did the work, I improved my times—and I started to win races again. That was a lightbulb moment for me. When I made the connection between doing the work and getting the result, making the commitment was easy. The competition started at training.

The following year, Katie Canning and Amy Townend weren't swimming at State Championships because they were at the Youth Olympics, but I swam and I did far better than I had the year before. I recorded personal bests in all my races, and won two gold medals. I understood for the first time that the work was part of the win.

Chapter Two

2013

'I don't know where I'm going from here,
but I promise it won't be boring.'

—David Bowie

For my whole life up to this point, someone has told me what to do. And that worked really well for me, to be honest. Somebody told me what to do and when to do it, and I followed their instructions. I followed them incredibly well. I'm now 28, nearly 29, and no one is telling me what to do anymore, and I'm not sure I like it. My life feels like it has no structure.

There's no structure to my body, either. I miss the physical routine. I was training 35 hours a week, conditioning my muscles, building strength, burning fat. It's brutal work. But if I'm no longer competing, what's the point? Why would

27

anyone do it—what's the motivation? It's not sustainable. My training has been tapering off for months now, and I can feel my super-strength draining away. It's just inevitable, I guess. If I'm not an athlete, I'm not an athlete, but the idea of losing that strength makes me nervous.

One of the first things I notice is that I don't sleep as well anymore. The thing about doing 35 hours of training a week is that you're so physically wrecked at the end of each day, you just hit the mattress and you're gone, but these days I'm finding it hard to get to sleep. I'm going to bed at the same time that I used to, nine-thirty or ten, but I find myself staring at the ceiling for a couple of hours, or surfing the internet on my phone. The frustrating thing is that my mind is tired at the end of the day, maybe more now than it used to be, but my body is pinging with energy that I haven't used up. I used to push my body to extremes in training, and I was almost always shattered as a result, but that exhaustion felt so much better than this. It felt healthier, somehow.

I can feel my body changing. I've had practically no body hair for most of my life—it was dissolved by the chlorine— and the hair that stuck out of my swimming cap at the nape of my neck was always a little crispy. I'm happy the crispiness is gone, but I'm less pleased that my body hair has grown back. I miss the silky-smooth swimmer's skin I used to have.

My body is looser, too. Just a little softer. The difference is minute right now, but I know it will get more pronounced as time goes on. The days when I could haul couches and dining tables with Luke without even registering the weight are over. Gone is that airy lightness of being that I would get when I tapered, just before a competition, that feeling of every lean muscle being perfectly connected. Gone too is that hypersensitive knowledge of my physical self, when any minor twinge told me something was out of place. I guess that's not a skill I need anymore.

I miss being strong. At my peak physical fitness, I could do 27 chin-ups. I threw weights around the gym like they were made of foam. I really loved that feeling. It's not the end of the world that it's gone, but being physically strong made me feel emotionally strong. I don't like feeling like I'm losing control. It's more than just the end result, the physical result—I miss the sense of purpose. I had a reason to be strong when I was swimming. There's no reason to do anything now. But I have to do *something*.

I'm not panicking yet. I assume something will come up and, sure enough, a short-term answer presents itself— one that is delightful to me, quite frankly. Shortly after my retirement, I hear through the grapevine that Channel 7 is recruiting for the next season of *Dancing with the Stars*. Laugh all you want, but I've always dreamed of being on *Dancing with the Stars*, a reality TV show where minor celebrities partner with ballroom dancing professionals and compete to be the most outstanding dance couple of the series. It's totally ridiculous and I *love* it. I know I'm a massive dork, but I don't care—I want to be on that show so badly. I have always loved dancing. It'd be a physical challenge that would be completely new to me, but I would be using my body again, pushing the boundaries of what it can do. As an added bonus, being on television would give me a public platform that might lead to other media opportunities. I'm an ex-athlete, so that's what I'm supposed to do, right?

Dancing with the Stars is relaunching in 2013 with the very handsome Adam Garcia as a new judge, which makes the whole thing that much more appealing. I ask my manager to look into it, and she comes back fairly quickly and tells me the season is cast and there is no budget for any more celebrity dancers. Devastating. 'They can pay me nothing!' I tell my manager, but she's not keen on that. 'They can pay me next to nothing!' I insist. As it turns out, this offer is too good for Channel 7 to refuse. At the bargain price of next to nothing, which is quite a bit less than my co-stars are getting paid, I am recruited into the thirteenth spot for the thirteenth season of *Dancing with the Stars*, set to air in October 2013.

It's not a good time for me to be working cheap. The investment fund that Luke established in 2010 is still young and relatively small, and all the money he makes is reinvested back into the business—and of course my income has dried up since my swimming career sputtered to an end. The change in our finances was sudden and stark, and not at all what we expected, because I've been riding a strong wave since the beginning of my career.

In hindsight, I hit the elite level in swimming at a good time, when the Australian public was most in love with the sport. I came up just after the Sydney Olympics, off the back of a golden era for the sport, when swimmers like Susie O'Neill, Sam Riley and Kieran Perkins were national heroes, winning gold medals in the pool and being great Australian role models when they were out of it. Swimming was broadcast on primetime television when my career was at its peak, which gave us a huge audience and a huge amount of corporate support off the back of that. I had a steady, comfortable income throughout my career, and never really had to worry about money.

But times have changed for Australian swimming, which means times have changed for Luke and me. It feels like the profile of the sport is sagging, because it no longer gets the same primetime broadcast slots, and advances in technology have fractured the audience. There's also the reality that some of the star athletes have misbehaved in public. Changes in racing equipment, such as the super-suit era of 2009, perhaps cheapened our record-breaking achievements. It's all about public perception, ultimately, and by 2013 it's clear that public interest in the sport has definitely waned.

Luke has always been anxious about my income because he works in finance—it's his nature to look to the future and plan ahead. Every bit of income I've earned up until this point has been a discrete chunk of money. I've never had a salary or a recurring payment for anything, and of course it's impossible to predict what contract or opportunity will come up in a month, six months or a year. I've been pretty blasé about it in the past, because money always came in, but Luke has been warning me since we got together that the good times wouldn't last forever. 'We've got a 30-year mortgage,' he would point out gently. 'You probably won't be swimming for 30 years.' I knew the sponsorships would drop off when my career ended, but I expected more of a taper than a cliff.

Luke's had a hard time over the years trying to get me to be financially responsible. The first time he suggested I think about reining in my spending, almost a decade ago, I was outraged. We had a very long, very spirited conversation about it while driving from Brisbane to the Gold Coast to watch the Indy 500. He's happy to wear threadbare T-shirts, I like buying nice things. I felt like I'd earned the money, so it was my right to spend it how I wanted. He was pointing out that it might be in my best interests to think a bit more long term. I have come around over the years, and not just because it's a smart thing to do. Luke and I are a team, which means I can't just run my own game. I have to respect his feelings too.

With my income drying up, it feels like we have less and less oxygen to live on. Luke knows what I have coming in, and can see the balance between our income and our outgoings flipping the wrong way. When he asks me to cut $300 out of the weekly expenses, I do it. When we have to cut another $100 a week, I do it. I trust him and I know he knows what he's doing, but nothing about this is fun. We're doing our best to live on a budget and make our savings stretch as far as possible. We never go out, we never buy anything, we're just trying to stay on top of the bills. But it slowly becomes clear that even a strict budget won't save us. Luke is looking into the near future and things are dark. We've come to the point where something has got to give.

We're sitting at the dining room table one night, in the home we'd built from scratch just eighteen months earlier, when Luke tells me we can't afford the mortgage repayments anymore. He doesn't want to alarm me, because we are asset-rich, but our cashflow is a serious problem. He takes a breath, sighs heavily. 'We have two options,' he says. We have a large chunk of money invested in the equities fund that Luke manages. We can sell out of the fund and clear our mortgage, which will take the financial pressure off, but if we do this we'll destabilise the business that Luke has been building up for years—the business we've been building, really, because as Luke says, my support has allowed him to pursue it. It's just not a great look for the manager of a fund to sell their shares, no matter what the circumstances, let alone for a fund that has been built on alignment with its clients. The other option we have is to sell the house.

My first instinct is to sell out of the fund. It's heartbreaking to have to think about selling our home, and the solid bricks and mortar around us feels so much more substantial than the abstract value of an equities fund. But the decision is about more than what I want. It's about supporting Luke the way he has always supported me. We've been together since we were kids. He was integral to my success as a swimmer, and I feel like it's my duty to back him now and give his business the opportunity to grow. I know that Luke feels like he's in a tough position, because we have been relying on my income for so long, and he's asking me to do something I don't want to do. It costs more to run the equity fund than we make from it—paying lawyers and accountants and covering admin costs is a drain on our finances right now— but Luke is committed to the long-term plan he's developed for the business, and I'm committed to him. It feels utterly surreal to be so cornered financially that we have to give up our home, but that's just how it is. We have to keep our heads above water.

Our decision to sell comes just as my run on *Dancing with the Stars* is about to start—my bargain-basement television debut in sequins and flesh-coloured tights. It's a bit surreal with everything that's going on at home, but the TV show still seems like the best option for me career-wise,

34

because right now it's the only option. It might not pay well but I hope it will lead to something that does.

I'm trying to reinvent myself, figure out exactly what I'm going to, but I feel great pressure to earn money because I've always been the primary breadwinner. I'm excited about the show, but it's also a life raft, something to cling to while the pressure at home begins to spiral. We're scraping the bottom of the barrel, living week to week with all this uncertainty, trying to stay positive, but I feel like I'm letting us both down. I decide to try to control what I can control, which right now is ballroom dancing.

I have roughly six weeks of training in Brisbane before the show starts broadcasting, and, being my usual competitive self, I throw everything I've got at it. I spend six to ten hours a day in a studio with my partner, Dannial Gosper, trying to master the basics of ballroom. *Dancing with the Stars* is my job and I'm determined to take it seriously. I know I have some serious opponents, too, a few type-A personalities and at least one fellow Olympian, who are all training just as hard as me.

Once shooting begins, I fly down to Melbourne every Sunday evening and I'm there until Tuesday, which leaves Luke pretty much by himself to get the house ready for sale. He's juggling the bills and trying to keep the wolves at bay while I'm learning the *paso doble*. It's ridiculous but it's an income, however small, so he's not complaining. He's just not having much fun right now. We've had to borrow money from his brother and his parents to tide us over until the house is sold, and the pressure is wearing us both pretty thin. At home, there is anger, frustration and an uneasy kind of resignation, but at least I get to escape several days a week and disappear into a world of tassels and fan kicks.

Swimming has given me a keen awareness of my body, so I can feel when I'm not doing something right and I can take feedback and transform it into the right moves. But I'm not used to doing so much physical activity on my feet, and the impact of working on the ground instead of in the water is exhausting. I have to guard my wrist, which is still not right and twinges when I'm pulled in certain directions. Some of the lifts are really challenging because I have to support my full weight in my arms and wrists, but I push through the pain.

I'm nervous about injuring myself again, but actually I'm fine. It's my dance partner who is injured, about four weeks into shooting, in a fairly devastating way. I land awkwardly on Danny's leg after a lift and his knee cops the full weight, tearing with the impact. He ends up having to have a full knee reconstruction, which is heartbreaking for a professional dancer. Meanwhile, they pair me up with another dancer, Carmelo Pizzino, because the television audience is waiting. It's pretty awful just to move on from Danny but I'm on task—I have a job to do. The show must go on and so must I.

The experience of being on television as a minor celebrity is bizarre, and I suddenly find myself uncomfortable in front of the camera, in a way that I never was when I was an Olympic swimmer. In week one I'm struck by horrible cottonmouth during my post-dance interview. I get better at the banter as the show goes on, but I never stop feeling uncomfortable. For me, the talking is a lot worse than the dancing; I'm good when my whole body is working.

Physically, I like my chances in this televised dance-off. I suspect a few of the bigger celebs in the competition are guaranteed to make the finals: they're the biggest names, they're undoubtedly getting paid the most money, and they're the people the audience most wants to see. But it turns out I'm actually a pretty good dancer, for an amateur, so I reckon I'll do okay. Eliminations start in the second week of shooting and people start dropping like flies, but I hang in there with a smile on my face, twirling through the cha-cha-cha, the tango, the samba and the jive, a fairly inglorious Lindy hop and a killer rumba. I make it all the way to the end of the regular competition, to week ten of the broadcast, before I am finally eliminated.

I'm disappointed that I don't get to compete in the Grand Finale, but I feel like week ten is still pretty impressive. The top three—Tina Arena, Rhiannon Fish from *Home and Away* and 'grand illusionist' Cosentino—are all professional performers who have been singing and dancing their whole lives. I came fourth, so technically I'm the best of the 'normal' people, the non-professional performers. Forever a competitor.

The day of the auction comes up in the middle of all this. Luke and I sit on the kerb outside, staring at our beautiful home and feeling utterly miserable. I suddenly register how much weight he has lost. He must have dropped 8 kilograms in three months, and he was pretty lean to begin with. It really hits me then how large a burden he's been carrying while I've been off dancing, and I feel angry with myself for letting us fall into this hole. I wish I had been more cautious with the money I made when I was swimming. Maybe we shouldn't have built a house at all. Maybe we shouldn't have built such a nice one. There are just so many things we could have done differently to avoid this shitty day. Then I remember that at least we have an asset to sell—it could be far worse. And at least the pressure will be off and we can start over. We're still in our twenties, after all.

We sit inside listening while the auctioneer runs the bidding, and the number climbs up and up, over our expectations. It's bittersweet because we really love this place, a beautiful, airy, modernist house built over a sloping yard in Seven Hills. He calls for final bids and then it's done, and we make our peace with moving on. But then, in the weeks following the auction, the weirdest thing happens—something our real-estate agent has never seen before. The guy who bought our house gets cold feet and pulls out of the sale, forfeiting his deposit, so we end up still owning our house and having some money in the bank, like it just dropped out of the sky. It's not a huge amount but it's enough to repay Luke's family and buy us some time to get back on our feet.

In addition to carrying me and Luke financially, being on *Dancing with the Stars* keeps me 'relevant', as my manager likes to say. It's awful but it's true. This is why celebrities go to red-carpet events and launches—to stay in the public eye. It increases your value as a media personality. I hate those high-fashion events. Some people love getting glammed up and going to parties, but it's just not my personality, and networking makes me uncomfortable. *Dancing with the Stars* is a great physical challenge and I can focus fully on that, but in the back of my mind I know that there's another purpose to this project, which is to get offered more work in the media.

I don't actually want to be a professional media personality, but I have no qualifications. What else am I supposed to do? I start working on my social media profile, trying to build up an audience, but I actually don't have much of a clue what I'm doing. My manager has all these rules for what and when I should post, but to me it feels inauthentic. I'm just trying to be myself, on TV and online, and hoping like hell it works out for the best.

I am in limbo about who I am and what I want to achieve in the next phase of my life and career—that's the real problem. I have no sense of direction; I'm just waiting to see what happens. This is difficult for anyone, but my entire adult life to this point has followed a very organised path, which was perfect for me. Right now I'm staring out into the fog, feeling uneasy.

2002

'Do or do not. There is no try.'

—Yoda

I knew that I wanted to swim and I wanted to win, and that made all the difference. I qualified for my age group in the National Championships when I was fifteen, and the following year, 2001, I qualified for two finals at the Open Nationals. A teammate at the club expressed genuine surprise at that. 'I didn't even know you were that good at swimming,' she said, which really got under my skin. It was my own fault for coasting under the radar for so long, but boy, was I going to show her. I was going to show everybody.

Every time I saw results, it made me want to train harder. Between fifteen and seventeen, I added a couple of extra training sessions a week to my program, and immediately

I saw improvements in my swim times and race finishes. My reputation as a 'rock lobster' would linger for quite a while yet. People didn't see me finishing all my laps and doing the work, because I now just blended in with the other teenagers who had been doing the work all along. I felt like they still saw me as someone who just turned up to meets as a social thing, who would never really amount to anything. There was definitely a lag between when my attitude changed and when people began to look at me differently.

I placed fifth in both my finals at the 2002 Open Nationals, and was selected for the junior national team as a result. I was going to represent Australia at the Oceania Championships in New Caledonia! It was an incredible moment, and a huge privilege. It was my first overseas meet as part of a team, not to mention the first time I had travelled overseas without my mum. She dropped me off at Brisbane airport—I was dressed in the junior national team uniform I'd been issued—and I set off for an adventure. Putting my toe in the water of international competition in this way was the starting point for the next decade of my life.

In the international departure lounge at Sydney airport, I met the rest of team, who had come from everywhere—Western Australia, Tasmania, South Australia. I felt an immediate sense of camaraderie, like being at the club but slightly more intense, slightly more thrilling. I was thrilled to be part of this group of kids who were absolutely at the top of their game. They loved swimming as much as I did. They had a talent for it, like I did. But we were young enough to be pretty lighthearted as we went into the competition. Swimming is a social sport, and I had always felt a kinship with the people I met who were into it, but there was definitely an extra edge of fun when we were all in it together, flying to another country to compete for our country. That's not to say I wasn't very focused on winning. I was there to race, first and foremost, but I still wanted people to like me.

There are always 'naughty' people on every team, and the New Caledonia crew was no exception. The thrill-seekers tend to drop off later in life as competition intensifies, but amongst the teenagers on that trip there was a fair number who were determined to stay up past curfew or get their hands on some alcohol. There was even a smoker in our ranks, though he didn't end up being all that good at elite level swimming. I didn't really get involved in any of those antics, but that's not to say I didn't have my own very teenage distractions.

I was now seventeen, and it wasn't lost on me that the boys on the team were all pretty handsome—and there was one boy in particular who caught my eye when I saw him at Sydney airport. His collar was turned inside out so I adjusted it for him, which he later described as the moment he fell in love with me. His name was Luke, and I thought he was sweet, even though he spoke painfully quietly and slowly. I found myself, with my manic energy, constantly wanting to finish his sentences. He came from Sydney, he had a brother, he was studying economics at the University of New South Wales and he loved swimming as much as I did. He was smart. He agreed with me that the vanilla ice-cream with black flecks of real vanilla bean that they served us for dessert one night was probably the greatest thing ever, but he may just have been trying to impress me. He was smitten, or so he told me later. But it struck me that we had the same sense of humour—goofy and immature—and that was really nice. I also noticed that he was ultra-intense when it came to swimming, far more so than me. I thought I was hungry to win, but he left me far behind.

Luke was named 'Swimmer of the Meet'; he did exceptionally well. He broke a couple of Oceania records and won a couple of races, and his relay team beat the other Australian relay team, even though they were meant to be the underdogs. That was a very big deal. I had a fantastic meet as well, pulling in a handful of medals and hitting a number of personal best times, but it was a steady kind of success, about what I expected. Luke was the superstar.

When I got home, I found that something had shifted inside of me. For the first time, I genuinely felt like I had a future in swimming, and that that was a serious and worthy thing. I had no concept of what that future might be, honestly. Even at seventeen, I would never have articulated the idea that I might one day be an Olympic gold medallist—that was still a total fantasy. But all of a sudden I had purpose, a drive to be better, to aim higher, and a sense that there was something truly great that I could do with my body in the water.

At that time I was training with John Carew (or Mr Carew, as he liked to be called) and his assistant, Glenda Radley, at the Carew Swim School in Brisbane, the team that had coached Kieran Perkins to his 1500-metre freestyle gold at the Atlanta Olympics in 1996. They were coaching Hayley Lewis as well, so they had some serious talent on the books. It was clear to me that they didn't see any huge potential in me, despite a strong showing in New Caledonia; perhaps they thought I'd only come this far because of my innate talent. I didn't understand this yet, but you needed far more than that to win at the highest level.

I didn't speak to Mr Carew or Glenda about my newfound determination because I was far too shy about it. Outside of my own head, I had no confidence at all, and there was no chance I was going to put my hand up and tell them the rock lobster had retired. The other pretty significant problem was that Mr Carew's was really a distance club—they trained swimmers for endurance competition. I was and always had been a sprinter, a fast-twitch-fibre athlete, which required a completely different type of coaching. We didn't do nearly enough sprint work at training, and my body didn't cope well with the long, hard stretches of kilometres on kilometres that we would do instead. Even at seventeen, I knew I should be doing heavier weights in the gym, fewer repetitions but with higher weights, whereas the distance training was all about lower weights and more repetitions. Anyway, for these and other reasons, I started looking for a new coach. And I found just the guy I needed, training at my school's pool.

My father, to his credit, took care of us financially. He paid significant child support, which meant that my sister and I could go to private school, which changed the trajectory of my life. It was at Somerville House, as a student on the swim team, that I first met Stephan Widmer. Stephan started coaching at Somerville House swimming pool early in 2002, just as my focus started to sharpen. Although I was still training with Mr Carew and Glenda, I swam at school meets and had the opportunity to watch Stephan working with other swimmers. He was a Swiss migrant and a man of few words, and a bit of an unknown in the Australian swimming community. He was previously a swimmer—he had made the Swiss national team in his day—but he had never trained an Olympic-level swimmer. He got his start as a coach in Australia when he turned up at Scott Volkers' pool and asked Scott if he could watch Susie O'Neill train for the Sydney Olympics. For some reason Volkers said yes, and he became Stephan's mentor. So Stephan had pedigree, but no major runs on the board.

It was clear to me that Steph was a professional—that he knew what he was doing. His results were evidence of that. Marieke Guehrer was in his squad, and she was going great guns with his coaching, swimming super-fast. She swam the same races that I did, and she was doing the kind of sprint-orientated training that I needed to do too. I started paying closer attention to Steph, and I think he was doing the same with me. While I was still with the other club, he and I had a couple of brief conversations by the school pool, and I decided he was a really nice person, then at some point during the year he complimented my racing at a school meet. I don't know if that was a calculated move on his part, but it worked on me. I felt like Stephan saw something in me that my other coaches didn't.

When I made the decision to leave Mr Carew and Glenda to move over to Stephan's team, I felt very strongly that it was my responsibility to deliver the news to them myself. I don't know why I was so determined about this, since I'd been happy to let Mum call Stephan and ask if I could start training with him, but I wanted to be a grown-up about it and that meant giving them the bad news myself. And I'm glad I did, because the conversation we had was a real eye-opener. Glenda and Mr Carew were genuinely disappointed that I was leaving because they had had plans for me, plans that involved the 2004 Athens Olympics. They were working to a monthly schedule with a whole lot of seasonal targets, but yes, they had seen my potential and they had planned to help me reach it.

I was stunned. No one had ever mentioned the Olympics to me, and I hadn't had the audacity to think about it myself.

And while I was busy making all these plans to find a coach who would take me seriously, it turned out I already had two coaches who were very ambitious on my behalf.

To have someone articulate a vision for me involving the Olympics was just incredible. I had a feeling I could do something exceptional in the sport, but I would never have been able to frame it like that. I hadn't achieved much in swimming at that point, so it was just an energy starting to build up inside of me, but the coaches knew. It's just a pity Mr Carew and Glenda didn't say something to me earlier. I don't know if they were trying to keep me humble or if they didn't want me to become complacent, or if they'd just neglected to mention their plans to me, but by the time we had this conversation my mind was made up. I stood on the pool deck in my swimmers and tracksuit, terrified but resolute, and told them that this had been my last training session at the club.

It was a hard day. I don't like letting people down and I don't like confrontation, but I knew it was the right decision. I was young but I was clear-eyed. I knew what I wanted to do.

By the end of 2002 I was training with Stephan at the Commercial Club in Fortitude Valley. There was no talk about the Olympics or any grand plans for my future, which was probably for the best. We started with modest goals. I was in my final year of high school and had already decided to take the following year off to focus completely on swimming, as I was hoping to make the Australian team for the 2003 World Championships.

A friend of Mum's was surprised to hear that I was deferring university to swim. 'Is she really that good?' he asked.

'I guess we'll see,' was all Mum said quietly.

The first thing I had to work through with Stephan was his heavy Swiss accent. I struggled to understand his instructions over the sound of my own exhausted breathing at the side of the pool, my exercise-addled brain fighting to comprehend his English. But what he did, in a very subtle way at first, was make me want to train more. We started with six or seven sessions a week, which was one or two more than I had been doing with my old squad, but a few sessions less than the rest of the team. He didn't throw me in the deep end; he stepped it up slowly and let my natural competitive edge do the rest. Just by being around other girls who were working a bit harder and seeing the results, I would start pushing up to that level. I was still quite young and goofy, but I was more ambitious than I'd ever been, and my teammates set a high bar. I was a late bloomer as a swimmer, a couple of years behind most young women in my racing achievements—there were so many girls who had made the national team at sixteen or seventeen—but I had faith that I would catch up.

The type of training the squad did was completely different to what I was accustomed to, but I took to it immediately. Stephan didn't have anyone on the Australian team at that point, but he created an incredibly professional environment for the squad. Everything felt different, from the way he set up each training session to the overarching program he developed for each of us. He focused on the quality of our training over the quantity, and he was consumed by technical details. His ability to recognise and correct a minor flaw in a swimmer's stroke could have a huge impact on their race. If you adjusted the position of your hand by a centimetre, you could hold more water in every stroke, which made you more efficient, which meant you wouldn't tire as easily and you could maintain your speed at the end of a race. He was so keenly analytical and insightful in understanding how different bodies moved through the water. It wasn't a one-size-fits-all approach—he saw how different bodies performed and he made specific adjustments for each swimmer. I had to adapt from the distance stroke I had been using—where I paused for a fraction of a second between the right and left stroke—to a continuous, powering movement.

Moving over to Stephan's squad felt like the best decision I had ever made. Physically, I responded well to the training, but we also connected as people. I immediately felt a trust in him that I had never felt with my other coaches. Stephan took all the thinking out of it for me—I just followed his instructions and I began to see exponential improvement.

Even after just a few weeks with him, my body felt radically different when I swam. He did specific training in kicking and pulling (isolated stroke work), which I had never done before. 'You have to get over the barrel, Libby,' he would tell me in his thick Swiss accent, meaning I should keep my elbow high and strong under the water, using my lats to power through with every freestyle stroke. We loved mimicking his accent, which was like Arnold Schwarzenegger's in *Kindergarten Cop*: 'Get over the barrel, Libby!' Our other favourite phrase of Stephan's came from our kick training in the butterfly. 'You have to get the undulation going!' he'd say, pronouncing it *un-doo-lay-shun*. It was pretty funny. But as much as I laughed, I know these tiny details would make all the difference in the world at an elite level.

I had only been with Stephan a couple of months when I finished high school. We had a very serious discussion about schoolies week on the Gold Coast, the traditional week-long blow-out for graduating students. Schoolies was a total bacchanalia of drugs and booze, and it was highly unusual for coaches to allow young athletes to go, but I was keen and Stephan agreed to it for some reason. The rationale for keeping swimmers away from schoolies was not so much the fear that these young athletes would be led astray as the fact that they'd be out of the pool for several days. At that level, there was already a heightened pressure around swimming, a sense that swimming was everything, which is incredibly intense for a young adult. As much as I wanted to win, there was some small, stubborn part of me that resisted the idea of giving myself over completely to swimming. I still wanted to be a regular seventeen-year-old, doing stupid eighteen-year-old things. Schoolies felt like an important rite of passage and I wanted to be part of it.

I hadn't been a complete angel up until this point. I had started going to parties when I was about fifteen, where I would regularly drink, and drink too much, every second weekend or so. For some of this time I was taking things easy in the pool, but even when my competition started to gear up, my teenage antics didn't have much of an impact on my swimming. My young body could take a bit of battering and still do just fine in the water, because teenagers don't seem to get hangovers. I suppose I thought I could carry on that way indefinitely.

I went to schoolies determined to have a very good time in the time that I had. Stephan had only signed off on a couple of nights on the Gold Coast, because I was due to compete at the Melbourne World Cup event just over a week later. As it turns out, two nights was plenty. I booked an apartment at Surfers International with my three closest girlfriends, right amongst the action, and Mum dropped me off at the entrance on Friday afternoon. Hours later, I was drunker than I had ever been in my life.

I can't say that it wasn't a good time. I had fun, hanging out with my friends. We snuck into Crown Towers at some point to meet up with some boys we knew, and we met a lot of other random boys on the street. I was still at a point in my life where I needed all the boys to like me, so I lapped up the attention. But so much of the night was a blur, and I can't recall how I got back to the apartment. The next morning I was violently ill. I started vomiting and thought I would never stop—it was five o'clock in the evening when the nausea finally subsided. At that point I started drinking again, because that's what you do at schoolies, though I was far less enthusiastic about it the second time around.

Mum picked me up on the Sunday afternoon so I'd be ready for training on Monday morning. I felt relieved when I got into the car—sheer relief that I didn't have to jump on that drunken carousel for another night. I couldn't imagine what my friends were going to be doing for the rest of the week, but I knew I didn't want any part of it. I felt like I'd poisoned myself. I got a fairly nasty cold in the days after schoolies, but still had to train, still had to swim. My sister got married the following weekend and I was still sick at the wedding, And while I didn't regret going to schoolies, I didn't ever want to do that to myself again. It felt like I'd got something out of my system.

The week after my sister's wedding was the World Cup meet in Melbourne, one of a series of events held around the world that focuses on short-course swimming, where the races take place in a 25-metre pool. There's a lot of prize money involved, so people came from around the world to compete, which made it a great training ground for swimmers to experience world-class competition.

Race practice is crucial—it's a completely different mental and physical experience to training, and any swimmer who wants to achieve greatness needs to be exposed to as much racing as possible. For example, one of the reasons the United States breeds such great swimmers is because they get to compete in high-level races all year round through their NCAA college system.

I saw a lot of the people at the World Cup meet who had been on the junior national team with me, including Luke, who I'd been flirting with on MSN Messenger ever since we left New Caledonia. I don't know if our online chat had an effect or if Luke had had a growth spurt, but when I saw him on the pool deck in Melbourne I was very impressed. *Hmm, Tricky got hot*, I thought to myself. We'd been flirting for six months but I hadn't thought all that much of it until he was standing in front of me, looking very lean, very tall and very tanned. I was looking forward to getting to know him much better at the swim camp we would both be attending after the meet, though I didn't have a clue just how hard and fast I was going to fall for him.

I had no expectations around how I would perform at the World Cup, but I had a great run. It was my first experience racing against elite swimmers in open competition and I didn't shy away from the challenge. I hit a significant personal best time and won silver in the 100-metre freestyle, but what I remember most about that meet was a conversation with my coach.

Before the 100-metre freestyle final, while I was warming up, Steph pulled me aside and had a word with me—his version of an inspirational chat. 'If you listen to me, if you work hard, if you focus, you won't know yourself as an athlete in twelve months,' he said. He didn't articulate any specific goals, and he didn't set any boundaries or expectations, but he gave voice to the feeling I had inside me. And because I respected him so much, his opinion carried huge weight.

Having Stephan express that belief in me was a very powerful moment. I trusted him, and it sparked a new level of clarity in me towards swimming. It was like schoolies and the World Cup represented two different paths for me. I could see where they both led, and that they were two very separate things, and I had to make a choice between them. That choice turned out to be very easy, though my friendships were challenged along the way and my social life all but evaporated. I was ready to make swimming my everything, no matter the cost.

Chapter Three

2014

'By replacing fear of the unknown with curiosity
we open ourselves up to an infinite stream
of possibility.'

—Alan Watts

I've had the same girlfriends since high school, but I've found it difficult to talk to them about the career anxiety I'm experiencing because I'm acutely aware that I've lived a very strange life up to this point. I really don't want to seem like I'm complaining when I've had such extraordinary opportunities and experiences, but it's so strange just sitting around after *Dancing with the Stars* waiting for something to happen. I talk about it with Luke, who is pretty understanding, but when I'm with my girlfriends I try to listen rather than talk about this stuff.

I begin to realise that a lot of people feel directionless a lot of the time. A lot of people feel unsatisfied with their careers and don't know what to do about it. So the way I feel isn't unique, but that doesn't make me hate it any less. If anything, I become more acutely aware of my own personality, and how important it is for me to feel like I'm driving towards something. As a swimmer, I had all this energy and passion pouring into one dream. The dream is over, but I still have the same energy and passion—I just don't have anywhere to channel it. I'm worried that I will never feel that sense of purpose again.

I start looking at degrees and tertiary courses, trying to find something that could light a spark inside me. A qualification would give me some credibility, I think. I don't want to be someone whose only professional qualification is that they used to swim good. I consider teaching, and I think I might like to study psychology, but both of those will take years of full-time study to finish, and I don't want to be starting a new career when I'm in my thirties. And we don't really have the money to put me through uni, so really those options are out anyway. In the end, I sign up for a massage therapy course and a personal training course because they seem like a natural fit, but even as I'm doing the online modules I'm feeling kind of blah about it. I can't really see myself doing massage therapy for a living, though I do have very strong hands. I feel like I'm on autopilot, just doing the logical thing.

Luke isn't pushing me in any particular direction. He lets me know I'm supported and tells me I should take my time to figure out the next step, but there's no urgency. All the fear and angst around my future is coming from inside me, churning quietly around the clock. My income is back down to virtually nothing, which I hate. I feel like I'm not contributing anything, and that makes me feel worthless, like I'm doing something wrong. Ironically, Luke still isn't bringing in much money either, he's just a lot more relaxed about it. He's a lot more relaxed about things in general.

The most difficult thing for him, I think, is that I've become a different person since I retired. When I was swimming I had a singular focus. I was so driven, so clear. All of a sudden, this new person has appeared in the relationship who is just careening all over the place. I'm indecisive, flighty, unsure of myself. I'm not the same person he married, and I feel like a lesser person than the woman he married. He'd never agree with that, but I'm sure he's frustrated. This didn't happen to Luke when he stopped swimming, because he had another passion—for commerce and finance—that was absolutely genuine. He made a smooth transition from one life to another, whereas I just keep walking into walls while I'm feeling my way around in the dark.

The uncertainty is a grind. Although we've managed to hold on to the house, we still don't know how we're going to afford it, or whether we'll have to put it back on the market. I don't know what I'm going to be doing every day or what I'm working towards. A lot of the time I feel like I'm just shuffling papers, trying to look busy. I don't know how to support Luke in growing his business, either. We aren't having a great time together, to be completely honest. The grind feels like it has spilt over to our relationship and now and we're just hunkered down like roommates, waiting for something great to happen.

In the end, *Dancing with the Stars* does the trick. I have a brief, terrifying waiting period where nothing happens, and then Channel 9 offers me a job as a health and wellbeing commentator on their breakfast show *Today*. Perfect! I love health and wellbeing. I've been an elite athlete most of my life, which makes me a credible expert on the subject, right? It lines up with the courses I'm planning to do, while also building my media profile, so it feels like the right career move. It has to be, actually, because it's the only job offer I've got.

In reality, I'm less of a health and wellbeing expert and more of a general talking head for hire. Starting in February 2014, I appear on a segment called 'The Grill' every Thursday—it's one of those conversation panels where they get a bunch of public figures together to express their opinion on topical subjects of the day. It's a great opportunity to be on television, to stay relevant, but also to have a regular commitment each week that I can build a schedule around. I'm so sick of floating.

It's a significant commitment—I have to fly down to Sydney every Wednesday night to be ready to film on Thursday, and then fly home again straight after the segment—but I'm happy with the constant travel because it feels at least like I'm moving, like I'm doing something useful with my time. It's actually kind of ridiculous, though—I mean, just the travel costs alone are crazy, given how much time I'm on screen. These networks must have money to burn. I'm supposed to be an expert on everything, too, or at least have a strong opinion, from childcare to tax cuts to the rising cost of bread. I'm somewhere between a celebrity and an ordinary person on the street, I guess, and the segment is just a regular conversation happening on public television.

It's not particularly hard. I don't feel completely natural in front of the camera, but I do have opinions that I'm willing to share, and most of the conversations are so lightweight it's like talking to my mum. I just get on with it, for the most part, and try not to think about the fact that this isn't really what I want to be doing. I still don't know what that is, so this will do in the meantime.

There's one conversation on 'The Grill' that really means something to me—around legalising marijuana. I can feel myself getting geared up for a very passionate chat that day, because I'm very strongly opposed to the idea. Medicinal marijuana may truly help people and should be accessible with support from proper medical professionals, but legalising it across the board is a terrible idea, in my opinion. I really believe it's a gateway drug to other substances that can cause massive harm. I've seen it firsthand in my own family.

My brother Stewart has suffered severe, ongoing physical and emotional damage from both alcohol and drug addiction; he's been through rehab several times and has ongoing mental-health issues that have only been compounded by drugs and alcohol. His experience has had a profound impact on my point of view. I remember lying in bed as a teenager smothering my head with a pillow while pounding techno floated up from my brother's bedroom all night long, wondering why he didn't seem to care that I had to get up at 5 a.m. for training. It was a constant struggle to ask him to be quiet, or to respect other people in the house, because he was always high and just didn't seem to care. It might seem like a minor thing in the grand scheme of things, but it caused me so much stress, and it was even worse for Mum. Also, Stewart seemed to hurt himself all the time, either falling down or getting sick because he was taking so many drugs or drinking too much. He fell over in the park once and knocked out his four front teeth. On another occasion he was beaten with a fence paling, which broke his collarbone. We found the paling the next day and there was a rusty nail attached to one end, so all we could think was: *Thank god it wasn't worse.*

Mum wanted to take care of Stewy and make sure he was safe, but the only way she could keep him there was by letting some really dodgy friends of his hang around as well, so when I was fifteen I was surrounded by a bunch of older guys who were often under the influence of drugs. I didn't know how heavily affected they were, but I knew they weren't right and it made me uneasy.

I could see how easy it would have been for me to follow my brother down that path, but something inside me really recoiled. The reality is that Stewy was struggling with a lot of deep personal trauma, and that was the real driver for his addictions, but drugs and alcohol gave him a means to express that pain in the most destructive way possible. I know Mum would have done things differently had she had her time over again, however I also know that she was doing the best she could under the circumstances.

There is not a lot of lightness to my brother's story, so it's really hard for me to be blasé about legalising recreational drugs, let alone taking them. This, I'm sure, is part of the reason why I don't spin off into partying when my swimming career ends, although I understand why other people do. I feel as lost and disoriented as any other elite athlete when the all-consuming training schedule stops. I know the feeling of having all this twitchy energy to burn and suddenly having all this time on your hands, not to mention the fact that you're no longer getting that daily bump of serotonin that comes from pushing your body to its limits. That's an actual physical high that athletes experience when they're training at an elite level, on top of which you get these occasional screaming rushes of dopamine when you win an Olympic medal. And the adrenaline coursing through your body—how do you replace that feeling? Some former athletes feel like drugs will fill that hole, give them an echo of that intense natural high, but I just can't go down that path. I don't think it leads anywhere good. Not for me, at least. I don't even drink.

I get a bit of blowback on social media for expressing my opinion about legalising drugs on 'The Grill', but it's surprising to me how little effect this has on me. I understand that everyone has a different opinion, because everyone has had different life experiences. And as much as I'm getting paid to take a position, I'm not actually that militant about any of the things we discuss week to week. I don't have any formal qualifications, I'm not an academic or a politician, there's no real reason why anyone should listen to me on most of these subjects, but I've been given a megaphone. I'm very conscious that it's a great opportunity for me professionally, but it also feels kind of lame. It's not like I can even do much research on each topic, because they give me the articles we're going to discuss when I'm in the make-up chair. Half an hour of frantic Google searches is usually the most I can do.

Every time I get my make-up done, I feel like I'm under a microscope. 'What's that?' a make-up artist will ask me, pointing at a minor imperfection. 'Oh, that's just a scar,' I'll respond. They'll raise their eyes, looking dubious. Almost every week when the concealer goes on, I get the same advice. 'You might want to consider a bit of Botox—you're starting to get wrinkles around your eyes.' Every week I feel like climbing up on a soapbox and shouting at them about how growing old is a privilege, and how Botox-pushing people like them are making things very difficult for older women everywhere. But I'm a people pleaser and I have to work with these people, so I don't get on my soapbox; I grin and laugh awkwardly and try not to feel too self-conscious.

This is one of the many reasons I start to think that television is not my passion. My particular role is easy, sure. There's no real preparation, I don't have to investigate stories or file reports, or do any of the hard work that journalists do, but I can feel myself sinking into this lightweight celebrity role and that's not necessarily what I'm looking for. *Easy* is not what I'm looking for. I need a serious challenge.

2003

'Rock bottom became the solid foundation
on which I rebuilt my life.'

—J.K. Rowling

I was plagued by respiratory issues my entire swimming career. The first time I competed at the World Championships, in Barcelona in mid-2003, I had severe bronchitis, triggering asthma that was aggravated by the swampy air of the indoor pool. My asthma had been diagnosed late in life, when I was fifteen, but I'd always had bad lungs. I was prone to bronchial coughs and colds, and I caught pneumonia when I was ten, which almost put me in hospital. When my swimming career started to gear up, the recurrent nose and lung issues got worse, and I ended up on a raft of preventive medications just to manage them from day to day, let alone when I pushed myself with hard training sets.

Barcelona was my debut on the world stage, so while bronchitis wasn't unfamiliar to me, it was the worst time for it to appear. It was terrifying knowing that I needed my body to perform at its peak and yet I was struggling to draw a decent breath. My mind was cluttered with negative thoughts: *I can't do this, I'm sick, I'm not worthy, I can't breathe, I will fail.* What I realised, ultimately, is that this was just something I had to deal with. There was no point trying to wish it away. There was no point looking at other swimmers and feeling frustrated that they didn't have to confront the same challenge.

Stephan caught me walking to the marshalling area for the heats for the 100-metre butterfly, coughing and spluttering and wheezing. We stopped in the hallway for our pre-race chat, the last word from the coach that every swimmer has before they go out on the pool deck. Usually a coach will tell you what to focus on in your race process— power off the blocks, driving through the first 25 metres, accelerating from 35 to 50 metres and so on. But there in the hallway, Steph said, 'There's only one thing I need you to think about, okay?'

I nodded.

'You're strong, you're fit, you're healthy and therefore you are fast,' he said. 'This is your power phrase. You focus on this and nothing else, until you race.'

I'm strong, I'm fit, I'm healthy, therefore I'm fast. This line became a mantra for me, and I would use it for the rest of my career, repeating it on a loop from warm-up until I climbed onto the blocks. I felt like a bit of a dag using it at first, but I couldn't deny that it worked. It silenced the doubts in my head, blew all the negative thoughts away, sharpened my mind like a knife. *I'm strong, I'm fit, I'm healthy, therefore I'm fast.*

I hadn't spoken to my father in months—he hadn't even called to say congratulations for making my first Australian team—so I was stunned to arrive at the pool in Barcelona one day and find him standing outside with his partner, Nilsen, the woman he left my mother for all those years ago. Through my shock I managed to comprehend that they had come to Barcelona to watch me swim. My father hadn't told me he was coming. I doubt my mother knew, or she would have told me.

Standing there outside the venue, I had a very brief exchange with my dad and his wife. As usual, our conversation was about swimming because we had nothing else to talk about. My father always told me I had to go into 'the cave of pain' when I was racing, which I think he lifted from a book. He meant that I should work hard and push my body to its limits, push the boundaries of what I thought was possible. I think it was well-intentioned and it wasn't completely off the mark, but he said the same thing to me every time I saw him and it got very repetitive, very quickly.

I didn't want to ask what my dad was doing in Barcelona. I didn't really want to hear it. I was polite and amicable in our brief exchange, but inside I was burning with frustration. My mum was there, of course, but she deserved to be. She had supported me and believed in me since day one. She had taken me to every training session and swim meet since primary school, always putting herself second so that I could follow my dreams. My father had barely been part of my life to this point. Yes, he had supported us financially, but that was it. From my perspective, it felt like he couldn't be bothered to be an actual parent to me, and yet somehow he felt it was okay to show up in Barcelona and ride the wave of momentum that was building around my swimming.

I didn't see or speak to my father again during that meet. I had to push my frustration away and focus on the competition—lock my mind into the race and swim. Battling bronchitis, with my newly minted power phrase on loop in my mind, I took home two bronze medals from the competition that year, one in the 50-metre freestyle and one in the 4x100-metre freestyle relay. It was a solid debut on the international stage, but there was so much further I wanted to go.

*

Stephan had a fierce belief in my ability, and I felt that. I felt the weight of expectation coming from him, but that expectation allowed me to grow and thrive, both as an athlete and as a person. He saw the athlete in me, the physical talent. But he also saw that I had the psychological make-up of a champion. His belief in me made me want to try harder, to be better, to become the person he thought I could be. He reminded me of Luke in some ways, with his analytical style and emotional dryness. He said exactly what was on his mind and didn't bother to sugar-coat it, but he didn't waste words. This meant he was very direct in correcting me and trying to improve my performance, but he was also quick to say positive things. His generous compliments gave me a lot of confidence, but I also responded well to the constructive feedback. He pushed me, and I tried to take it to another level each time I swam.

We didn't talk in any weighty, meaningful way about the Olympics. It was the next major international meet, and so the next obvious step, but I think Stephan was careful in how he approached the subject. There was no additional pressure—at least not at first. We just moved on to the next goal, and that was the team for the 2004 Athens Olympic Games.

For me, the Olympics wasn't strictly the goal. All I wanted was to do better than I had done before, so at the end of 2003 I wrote down a time for the 100-metre freestyle that I wanted to achieve: 53.6 seconds, which was a full second faster than my personal best at the time. It also happened to be 0.1 second faster than the then world record. I wrote the number on a scrap of paper in fluoro pink pen, and scribbled a quote beneath it.

I've always loved inspirational quotes. I kept a notebook full of my favourite quotes and carried it around with me—it was filled with things that made me feel powerful or inspired or motivated. Some of them just made me laugh, like 'Don't get your knickers in a knot. Nothing is solved, it just makes you walk funny.' And my all-time favourite was 'They never said it would be easy, they just said it would be worth it,' which resonated with me because it seemed so universal. Life is hard, and there are always challenges, but there are always moments that make those challenges worthwhile. My whole swimming career was building up around that idea—that after the pain came the pay-off.

On the scrap on paper, beneath the number 53.6, I wrote: 'Whatever happens, happens for a reason and will be for the best in the long run.' I stuck the note next to my bed so it was the first thing I saw every morning when I woke up and the last thing I saw before I went to sleep.

After Barcelona, I started doing ten training sessions a week. Under the influence of Luke, who'd become my boyfriend, I'd also started doing some heavy core and cardio sessions every day. He and I had started a long-distance relationship after the 2002 World Cup; during the run-up to Barcelona and during my training for Athens, I was down in

Sydney every second weekend visiting him. He was obsessive about his exercise regime, extremely demanding of himself, and I found myself trying to mirror him when I was not in the pool. I added two 30-minute sessions on an exercise bike to my routine, increasing the resistance every five minutes. This made my legs stronger, as well as increasing my cardio-vascular fitness. I also added a 20-minute ab and core workout to my routine four days a week, in addition to the weights training prescribed by Stephan and my gym coach Stewart Briggs, which involved long sessions of plank holds and at least 500 crunches in every session. The extra training load gave me an edge, physically and mentally. I knew I was doing more than was required of me, maybe more than my competitors, and that gave me an extra layer of confidence.

I didn't have hard boundaries around what I wanted to achieve. The race time I wrote down was a goal which kept me on track, but I'd set no deadline for when I had to achieve it. I just knew that if I worked systematically towards being stronger and faster, and I eventually made that time, I would make it very bloody hard for anyone else to beat me.

When the National Championships came around in March 2004, which served as the Olympic trials, I was the leanest I'd ever been. I weighed a couple of kilos more at nineteen than I had when I went to the Oceania Champion-ships a couple of years earlier, but my skinfold measurement was completely different—I was skin wrapped around muscle. Instead of sitting heavy, my body aquaplaned in the water, gliding over the surface with every powerful stroke, my legs stronger than they had ever been. I was a far more efficient machine.

Form aside, I wasn't looking my best. I had developed a horrible rash just before the trials, pityriasis rosea. It wasn't itchy but gave me welts from head to toe, which made me feel incredibly self-conscious when I was walking around in bathers. Stephan had a knack for reframing things that got me out of my own head. 'It's just your speed rash,' he joked. 'It's going to make you go fast.' He honestly made me feel better.

We spoke just before the semi-final of the 100-metre free-style, our standard pre-race pep talk, but he took a slightly different approach. There was no advice to hold back and keep something in reserve for the final. 'Just go after it,' Stephan said, casually. 'Go out there, have fun and see what you can do.' I think Stephan had an inkling that I was on the verge of something special, though he wouldn't have said explicitly what that was. He wanted to open a door in my mind and let me look through it. He was incredibly crafty that way, a bit of a puppetmaster. If he had actually told me what he thought might happen, the pressure would have been unbearable. Instead of pointing directly at the goal, he just cleared the path and told me to run.

All of my work—the sweat, the grit, the focus—paid off in that semi-final. I hit my number three months after I wrote it down. I swam the 100-metre freestyle in 53.66 seconds, breaking the world record. In the stands, Stephan turned to Luke in his usual understated way and pointed at the scoreboard. 'Look at what she's done,' he said.

It was an extraordinary achievement, no doubt about it. It was the crowning glory of my career so far, and it gave me the greatest rush I had ever experienced as an athlete, a feeling of immense power, but the moment was precarious and short-lived. I broke the world record in the semi-final, but I didn't win the event. Jodie Henry took the gold medal in the final. She swam in under the radar, only a millisecond slower than my record-breaking time, but faster than me in the race that counted. Somehow, the media totally missed this part of the story. In my head, I was just relieved and grateful to have qualified for an individual event at the Olympics. I was aware that there was really nothing between Jodie and me. But in the media I was the golden girl, and Jodie barely rated a mention. I was the world record holder in the 100-metre freestyle, and that quickly became a millstone around my neck.

The problem with being the world record holder in any particular race is that you're the implicit favourite any time you swim. While I'd had a perfect race at the trials, I was going into the world's toughest, highest-profile swimming event with no experience at that level, and a massive weight of expectation on my shoulders. I was only nineteen, and it felt like I hadn't really done anything of note at that stage, and suddenly I was under a microscope. I tried not to read the newspapers or watch television reports, but it was hard to shut that stuff out completely, and every time the media mentioned my name the words 'world record holder' followed. I thought I was bulletproof and that the pressure wasn't getting to me, but that was a product of youth and arrogance more than anything else.

The Australian team flew into the town of Sindelfingen, Germany, for a two-week-long staging camp ahead of the Games. I imagined that I was dealing with the intensity of what was about to happen, but in retrospect it was in Germany that the cracks first started to show. I was missing Luke horribly and I was highly emotional. I felt overwhelmed and teary, completely volatile in my emotions, and if I couldn't speak to Luke every night—if training ran late or I missed the window between our two time zones—I'd be distraught. It wasn't until later that I appreciated how hard this was for Luke. He had swum at trials but failed to make the team, and desperately wanted the opportunity I had at that moment, but he was doing his best as a young boyfriend to support me. To his credit, I never sensed any bitterness or resentment from him at all. In fact, I was deeply paranoid that he would leave me, for reasons I couldn't rationally explain.

I didn't have the maturity to process what I was going through, and it only escalated when we arrived at the

Olympic Village. Even without the added pressure I was feeling, the Olympics are a beast of a thing. The intensity of your reaction—the intensity of the opportunity—is crippling. But at the same time, it was the most alive I had ever felt. The energy, the hype, the excitement of being in that moment, which comes around just once every four years, which everyone around you has been working towards for most of their lives, was absolutely electrifying. Everything was so extreme, I felt like I was on a roller-coaster.

We arrived in our Australian Dolphins uniforms and joined a flood of athletes from around the world, and from that moment everything started to feel slightly surreal. The enormous village precinct included miles of apartments and residential buildings for the athletes, an international food hall the size of two football fields, a games area, a gymnasium. The layout in Athens felt like a hodge-podge, and the landscaping was unfinished, so the buildings looked like they'd been erected in fields of dirt. When we arrived at our apartment, the plumber was still installing the toilet and the shower had no lip or screen, so water ran out under the bathroom door.

I shared the apartment with six or seven girls from the Australian swimming team, and each of us had our own weird habits. Some hid in their rooms in isolation, while the rest of us hung together in the lounge room and watched TV. Some were single, others had partners. Some were constantly buried in books, and some—like me—were a bundle of nerves. But we all had the same hairless skin and chlorine-bleached hair at the nape of our necks. We were all incredible athletes. We were all ready to compete at the pinnacle of our sport.

It was amazing to walk into the food hall and see so many different types of bodies, each shaped by their sport. There were seven-foot-tall volleyball players and tiny, muscular gymnasts. The weightlifters always hulked over two stacked plates of food, and the distance runners were all lean and wiry. The shooters just looked like regular people, with regular untrained bodies. I saw plenty of famous athletes who I only knew from TV, and felt that little rush you get from breathing the same air as a celebrity. It was fascinating, bizarre and a tiny bit terrifying. These were the best of the best—and my competitors were out there somewhere too. I enjoyed people-watching but before the competition I was very aloof. I stuck with my housemates—unless I saw a bunch of athletes wearing the Australian uniform, and then I would walk right up and say hello. I was totally comfortable sitting down to eat with strangers if I knew they were on my team.

The excitement helped my nerves a little, but there was no denying the mounting gravity of the situation, which was triggered just a little more by the general disorganisation in the village. Our Greek hosts were incredibly lax with the schedules for the buses that would ferry us to the competition sites. I liked things to be a certain way when it came to competition. I liked to control everything I possibly could until the moment I stepped onto the block, so I struggled with that lack of control, of not being where I was supposed to be when I wanted to be there. And some days everything ran on time, which only made things worse, adding to my stress. I had no way of knowing which way the dice would fall on the days I was going to compete.

Our team qualified for the final of the 4x100-metre freestyle relay on the first day of competition. On paper, we weren't the best team—the Americans were without a doubt the favourites—so the noise in my head, the expectations, had quietened down a little. As I walked to the marshalling area for the final, I was listening to Gloria Estefan's 'Reach', the closing ceremony song from the 1996 Olympic Games in Atlanta. I tested my goggles, pulling at the straps, and felt them snap in half in my hands. I was carrying a second pair with me, something I'd never done before, so I felt like luck was on my side.

I really loved my team. Jodie Henry, Petria Thomas and Alice Mills were so energetic, warm and positive that it was a joy to swim with them, and I think it was quite disarming for our competitors to see the lightness we brought to the meet. This helped me keep my anxiety in check because it was about the team, not me. The load was spread, which made it easier to bear.

On the first day of my first Olympic Games, we broke the world record in the 4x100-metre freestyle relay and won a gold medal—the first time an Australian team had won the race since 1956. Alice led us off and I swam the second leg, before Petria and then Jodie smashed it home. She had an epic back-end speed. We looked up as she hit the wall and saw the result sky high on the scoreboard. Australia, 3 minutes 35.94 seconds, in the number-one spot. The achievement made my heart burst. It felt like all of that punishing work—the crunches, the bike sessions, the hours and hours in the pool, the exhaustion, the sacrifice—was worth it. I had stepped up onto the world stage and done something truly extraordinary, and I was beaming as I took to the podium beside my teammates with my first Olympic gold medal hanging around my neck. When the Australian anthem started to play, all four of us wept with joy.

The only thing is, in the back of my mind, I knew I hadn't swum my best race. I put us in the lead in my leg but something felt a bit off, like it just wasn't my day, and I wondered retrospectively if we had mistimed my taper. Throughout training, you work at a break-neck pace, punishing your body, day in, day out. But three weeks before competition you begin to back off, reducing your workload to allow your body to freshen up for peak performance in competition. If you mistime your taper, you either peak too early and start feeling shabby during the competition, or you don't quite have time to get to your peak. I think I fell slightly short of my peak, and I just felt like I could have done better.

Something was brewing, I just couldn't see it. It was an unease, just out sight. Maybe it was the bad taper, maybe it was the pressure, but it was about to make itself known.

Everything had happened so quickly. I hadn't thought, in the lead-up, that it was my time to win a gold medal in an individual event at the Olympics. I hadn't even won a gold medal at a national level, but that world record–breaking swim had sped everything up—in my mind and in the eyes of the world. I felt like I was locked on to a path, moving too quickly, but unable to do anything but push forward. I wasn't in control.

In retrospect, so many things were off. Athens was only my second major international meet with Stephan, so he and my gym coach were still learning how my body responded to things. And I was learning what it meant to compete at that highest level, working in an extremely intense environment that was pushing me to the limit. I assumed my taper was off during the relay, but I also thought it would get better the next day. I was running on blind faith.

The heats for the 100-metre freestyle were on day five of competition. The buses that afternoon were off schedule again, running at least 40 minutes behind, and I was frantic as a result. I wanted to get to the pool at least two hours before my race so I could spend the first half-hour stretching and listening to music, just chilling out. I wanted to get into the warm-up pool an hour and a half before my race and do my laps, drills and exploding starts to activate the lactic acid in my body and get my fast-twitch muscle fibres firing. I needed time to have a long, hot shower afterwards and stretch out my muscles, before getting into my race suit and heading to the marshalling area. I needed time to walk through my routine, my preparation and my process. And most importantly, I needed time to acclimatise to the atmosphere at the pool. I hated feeling rushed.

But the bus was late, so my routine was off and I failed to adapt to the change and roll with the punches. Jodie was waiting beside me, calm and collected. She was watching me closely; I learned years later that my agitation actually made her confidence soar. The warm-up was important, but it wasn't the be all and end all—Jodie knew that. Our bodies were so finely honed and trained, over years and months, that the twenty minutes of exercise directly before a race would not determine who won. It was far more important to be mentally focused and adaptable—to let your body do what it had prepared for.

I got to the pool an hour and fifteen minutes before the first race, so I had no time to acclimatise—I had to jump straight in the warm-up pool and go. And for the rest of that evening I felt like I was out of sync, and unable to control my emotions. I didn't have the capacity to calm myself. What I really needed was to take three minutes to stop and breathe, but I just couldn't do it. I felt like I was racing against the clock and falling behind every step of the way. In reality, I was trying to hold on to something that I didn't actually have. I thought I had the gold medal in my hands and it was somehow slipping out of my grasp, but that was an illusion.

The heats for the 100-metre freestyle were unremarkable. Heats were a muscle work-out, a kind of low-intensity warm-up, and relatively little effort was required. I didn't notice anything grossly out of whack because I wasn't searching for my top gear, but I'd been feeling nervous and agitated all day, far more nervous than I should have been.

When I dove into the water in my semi-final, I knew something was wrong. I just didn't seem to have any power—in my legs, in my arms. I was reaching for something in my body that wasn't there. I felt uncoordinated and lacking drive, like a crucial gear I needed just wouldn't engage. The emotion I was feeling, more than anything else, was confusion. When I touched the wall and turned to the leaderboard, my confusion turned to devastation. I had placed fifth, too far down the ranks to secure a position in the final. It was like a punch to the gut and I felt absolute shock, like the floor had just dropped out from underneath me.

Ultimately, I missed a place in the final by just 0.09 seconds. I was the world record holder and I couldn't even make the final—the embarrassment was crippling. I made my way out of the pool towards the media scrum, where Kieren Perkins was waiting, then the swimming correspondent for

Channel 7. 'You must be disappointed,' he said, and I felt my face flush. The second semi-final race had started as I was walking away from the pool, and it finished as I stood beside him fumbling for words. And what happened, as I was standing there in front of the camera drowning in self-pity and shame, was that Jodie Henry broke the world record. She broke the record that I had made just months before, by 0.14 seconds. Records are made to be broken—that's just the way things go. But in that moment it was like a left jab followed by a right hook. I hadn't made the Olympic final and my best achievement had been eclipsed by my biggest rival.

I was sitting in the stands the following night when Jodie won the gold medal for the 100-metre freestyle. I was an absolute mess, but I forced myself to switch gears. I had to reset, because I had another race to swim—the 50-metre freestyle. Stephan wanted me to watch Jodie's race because he knew it would be an important learning experience for me. He wanted me to be inspired to be in that final four years into the future.

I also wanted to support Jodie in her golden hour. She may have been my rival but she was also my teammate— she deserved to have my backing. When she won the gold, I desperately wanted to be happy for her, but I was so gutted that I struggled to get there. I cheered for her from the stands, but my heart was hard. What it did was fuel my hunger to win.

When I swam the 50-metre freestyle two days later, I was out to prove that I deserved to be there. The gold medal win in the relay hadn't been a fluke—my teammates weren't carrying me. I had come up short in the 100-metre freestyle, but on this night I won a bronze medal in my own right. I was one of the top three swimmers in this event in the world. In the face of failure and embarrassment, I had locked down, stepped through my process as an athlete and come through, and for the second time at the 2004 Olympic Games I stood on the podium with a medal around my neck.

I felt I had proved in that moment that I could come back. Next time, I would come back even stronger.

Chapter Four

2014

'Everybody is a genius. But if you judge a fish
by its ability to climb a tree, it will live its
whole life believing it is stupid.'

—Albert Einstein

My name is Libby Trickett and I'm a talking head
on Australian breakfast television, a one-time celebrity
dancer on *Dancing with the Stars* and, as of early 2014,
the National Channel and Partner Manager for Megaport,
an Australian internet technology company. I have the
Megaport company sales pitch down cold: 'Megaport is a
layer 2 point-to-point connection service connecting data
centres. We maintain ports in all data centres, enabling
virtual cross connections for our clients over dark fibre . . .'
I've been in the job a couple of months now, and the words

89

just roll off my tongue. Unfortunately, I have no idea what they mean.

I have a meeting with a client in a remote business park in the northern suburbs of Sydney, and the ride out there takes forever. For a solid half an hour, I huddle in the back seat of a taxi and mull over how completely and utterly out of my depth I am. This is the first sales meeting I've had without a Megaport engineer by my side, and I'm genuinely terrified. I've done this just enough to know exactly how much I don't know, which is worse than going in completely cold. Ignorance is bliss, right? I have zero bliss right now.

The plan is that I'll write down any tech questions the client might have and get back to them with answers at a later date. Meanwhile, I'll tell the client everything I know: 'Megaport is a layer 2 point-to-point connection service connecting data centres. We maintain ports in all data centres, enabling virtual cross connections for our clients over dark fibre . . .' I'm not even sure what dark fibre is, to be honest. The only fibre I'm familiar with is dietary.

At reception, I am met by a senior manager, who tells me other team members are on the way to join us. 'Debra is so excited to meet you!' he says.

'Oh, great!' I smile broadly, dying a little inside.

'She's such a big fan!'

'Oh, is she? That's so nice!' Debra is in for a disappointment, I reckon.

My mum, Marilyn, my brother, Stewy, and me, still not even a year old, in 1985.

Hanging with my siblings Stewy, Justine and Victoria in 1986.

Playing with the big kids in 1987—even when I was two I was competitive!

Me in 1988. Growing up, our world seemed to be built around water, whether it was swimming at home, going to the beach, or hanging out along The Strand in Townsville.

Rome, 1993. Mum took us on a trip around Europe all by herself.

Staying at the Dockside Apartments, Brisbane. A small-town kid in the big city, heading to the 1995 State Championships.

Me (left), competing against Sarah Bowd and Tanya McDonald at the State Primary School Championships, 1996.

At the Brisbane School Metros, 1997.

The final day of high school with my best friends, Jess, Casey and Leith, who I met there on day one.

Breaking the world record in the 100-metre freestyle at the National Championships in 2004 in a time of 53.66 seconds. This was the crowning glory of my career so far and the greatest rush I had experienced as an athlete. How about that facial reaction?! *(Nick Laham/Getty Images)*

So young and so in love—me in 2004 with Luke Trickett. We'd met at Sydney airport on our way to the Oceania Swimming Championships two years earlier.

Day one of the 2004 Athens Olympics. I couldn't have dreamed of a better way to start my first Olympic Games. First event: a world record and a gold medal shared with Petria Thomas, Alice Mills and Jodie Henry. *(Chris Ivin/ Getty Images)*

Winning bronze in the 50-metre freestyle at Athens and hugging my idol, Inge de Bruijn of the Netherlands, who won gold. After a rollercoaster week of competition, this was a great moment. *(Greg Wood/AFP/ Getty Images)*

Melbourne Commonwealth Games, 2006. This was a personal highlight: winning my first 100-metres freestyle gold at an international competition. *(Ross Land/Getty Images)*

With Jodie Henry and Alice Mills after winning the 50-metre freestyle—
my fifth gold—at the 2006 Melbourne Commonwealth Games.
(Phil Walter/Getty Images)

It was a crazy
day, but we had
a lot of fun at
our wedding in
2007.

Taking off for the 100-metre butterfly at the 2008 Beijing Olympic Games. *(Tim Clayton/Sydney Morning Herald)*

Leading the pack in lane four on my way to gold in the 100-metre butterfly in Beijing, with American Christine Magnuson (silver) in lane five and fellow Australian Jessicah Schipper (bronze) in lane three. *(Adam Pretty/Getty Images)*

Celebrating after the race with my coach, Stephan Widmer.
(Martin Bureau/AFP/Getty Images)

The 100-metre butterfly gold medal presentation. No words can describe the relief, but this picture almost captures it. *(Natalie Behring/ Bloomberg/Getty Images)*

This was the best part—
celebrating with Luke.
(Mike Hewitt/Getty Images)

Congratulating Britta Steffen after she won the 100-metre freestyle in
Beijing. I took silver. *(Greg Wood/AFP/Getty Images)*

Bronze in the 4×100-metre freestyle relay in Beijing: Melanie Schlanger, Alice Mills, Cate Campbell and me. *(Adam Pretty/Getty Images)*

With Emily Seebohm, Leisel Jones and Jessicah Schipper receiving the gold for the 4×100-metre medley relay on the final day of competition. Nothing better than singing your national anthem with three amazing women. *(Jeff Gross/Getty Images)*

Celebrating our record success at the Beijing Olympics with all of the
Australian female swimming medallists. Top (left to right): Shayne
Reese, Kylie Palmer, Bronte Barratt, Stephanie Rice, Linda Mackenzie,
Emily Seebohm, Felicity Galvez, Angie Bainbridge. Bottom: Lara
Davenport, Tarnee White, me, Leisel Jones, Jessicah Schipper.
(Milan Scepanovic/Newspix)

Returning home after Beijing to the Sydney tickertape parade along
George Street. *(Craig Golding/Sydney Morning Herald)*

With Mum and Luke after announcing my first retirement at the end of 2009. *(Charmaine Wright)*

Trying to transition to life after sport: presenting at the 2010 Pan Pacific Swimming Championships on Channel One. *(Mark Chapman)*

Returning to swimming for my third Olympic Games, London 2012. We won heat two of the 4×100-metre freestyle on day one and the team would go on to win in the final. *(Clive Rose/Getty Images)*

Mental illness has many faces. This was me in the midst of my darkest moments of postnatal depression. Poppy was only eight months old.

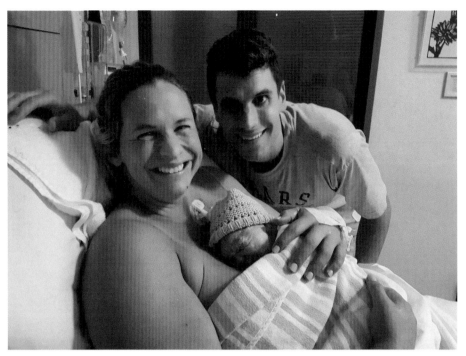

Moments after the birth of our second daughter, Edwina Daisy, in 2018. I was completely in shock that we had another girl!

Poppy meeting her baby sister for the first time. Heart explosion central!

They usher me into a sterile boardroom—white walls, white table, in an office park in the middle of nowhere— and three representatives from their company sit down to listen to my spiel. Debra isn't one of them; it turns out that she works for HR. The three men in front of me know who I am, but I'm not sure they care. They're perfectly pleasant, warm even, but they're here for business. And I'm here to win their business with my trusty sales pitch. *Ports! Data centres! Dietary fibre!* Only the anxiety has clamped on my chest like a vice and I feel like I'm having a panic attack.

One of the men in the room is the client's digital technology manager, and he has some questions. If he's going to buy virtual cross connections from Megaport, he'll need to know the system capabilities. It's a new product and he's not familiar with the specifications, though, as it quickly becomes apparent, he's not alone. He asks me a question, I say I'm sorry I don't know the answer, and I write it down for our engineers. He asks me a question, I say I'm sorry I don't know the answer, and I write it down. This goes on for about half an hour, the most uncomfortable 30 minutes of my life. He is a highly competent technology manager and knows exactly what he needs to know, whereas I am an incompetent fraud who is wasting his time. It's clear I don't know anything about the product I'm trying to sell them. I barely understand the questions he is asking, and the best I can do is smile, apologise and write his questions down. Someone at Megaport understands this stuff, just not me, which begs the question—what am I doing here?

Bevan Slattery is a serial entrepreneur who has a string of successful start-ups to his name. I know him from the swimming world—his kids swim at St Peters, where Luke used to swim, so we're part of the same family. Bevan is a patron of the club and has donated quite a lot over the years to support its Olympic hopefuls, but I don't meet him until my career is over. We're introduced at a welcome home party for the swimmers who went to the London Olympics, and Bevan takes a shine to me. He says he likes my energy. A year later, when I have announced my second and final retirement from swimming, Bevan and I reconnect. He sees me on *Dancing with the Stars* and has decided he wants to give me a job at his new tech company. Qualifications are clearly not high on the agenda, because I'm not qualified to do anything except swim and, at a stretch, dance on television. 'It's about getting the right personalities in the right business,' Bevan explains. I can only assume he knows what he's talking about.

And actually, yeah, I think I'm ready for a job. I have my weekly five-minute guest spot as a commentator on the *Today* show, but it doesn't feel quite right. I know sportspeople often transition to media careers, but I feel like an imposter and I'm tired of the spotlight. It's been intense, these last few years. I want to get out of the public eye and live a normal life, connect with normal people and do normal things, like working in an office. At least, I think that's what

I want. I'm still trying to figure it out. Anyway, under the circumstances, Bevan's job offer seems like a great idea.

Around the same time my nascent morning TV career kicks off, I join Megaport, Bevan's latest business venture. It's a sales role, three days a week, pitching a new and fairly niche internet technology to businesses that already use fairly complex internet technology. There are twelve people who work at Megaport, and every one of them except me has been in the tech industry their entire adult lives. They understand the product. I can switch my computer on and post pictures on Instagram—that's about the extent of my technical expertise.

This is a start-up, so there's no formal training. We're clustered around trestle tables, sitting on second-hand chairs, and everyone is kind of making it up as they go along. It's a sink-or-swim scenario. My colleagues seem to be on top of things, at least partly because they're knowledgeable about the industry we're operating in, but I came into the job expecting to be told what to do, and yet I'm pretty much left to my own devices. I'm expected to have ten face-to-face meetings a week with potential clients, which sounded fine to me initially, like a long series of coffee dates. I like people and I like coffee, I figured. I can go and meet people and chat to them. And surely they'll just buy things from me because I'm charming . . .

But then reality strikes. Who am I actually supposed to be having coffee with? I'm expected to make twenty sales calls a day, but I don't even know who to call. Seriously, who do I *actually* call? Who am I supposed to be meeting with? And, come to think of it, what am I supposed to say? I have a list of leads that the team has cobbled together but it's incomplete and unreliable, and leads to more dead ends than actual clients. And I'm not sure how to find more. If I was a go-getting self-starter who's hungry for success, I could probably make do, but right now I really need someone to hold my hand, because I have no clue what I'm doing.

It's not just that I have no experience in this job—I have no experience in *any* job. I've never worked nine-to-five. I haven't had to sit still for eight hours since I was in school, and back then I could at least run around on the oval at lunchtime to blow off steam. Speaking of lunchtime—I'm not entirely sure when that's supposed to happen. Do I just get up and leave when I feel like it? Do I have to ask permission to go to the toilet? I'm almost 30 years old but this is a legitimate question I have. I genuinely don't know.

I discover that I don't learn well by sitting still. At first I'm fidgety and I just want to get up and move my body, but I soon start to feel fatigued and lethargic. It's not the satisfying exhaustion I used to feel after a training session, it's the kind of tiredness that you get from information overload—you feel it in your eyes and your neck. And because I'm not in training, and I'm bored and frustrated, I treat myself to KFC every second day for lunch, and eat chocolate every day for that midafternoon pick-me-up, which is a disaster.

The job takes a toll on me physically, and that only makes me feel worse.

My lower back in particular really hates Megaport. Sitting in a chair all day makes it absolutely scream, and I'd kind of like to scream too: *This is no way to live, people!* I can't believe people spend their entire adult lives sitting at desks all day long, day after day. How will I survive it? I have scoliosis and naturally weak glutes—they were always a problem in training—and both of those things seem to be amplifying the problem, which leaves me in a low-grade kind of misery. I'm not going to die, but I am sore and uncomfortable most of the time, and it's only getting worse.

If I'm not at my desk, I'm on a plane flying down to Sydney for my weekly TV spot, or sitting in a hotel room, or in a make-up chair. It occurs to me that I have to increase my incidental exercise, but how do you fit that in when it's not your actual job? I need to do it for my mental health, as well. I'm not good when I'm not exercising. And being out of shape just compounds this feeling that I'm not in the right place and I'm not doing the right thing. Megaport isn't spiritually nourishing, and it isn't good for me physically. It's just something I have to do, mostly because we need the money.

One small blessing is that Megaport is across the road from the pool where I used to train, and there are quite a few people on the team who are keen swimmers. We get a bit of a lunchtime swim club happening and head over the road once or twice a week for a swim. In Sydney, when I fly down to shoot my *Today* segment, I catch up with one of my colleagues from *Dancing with the Stars* for a dance lesson, which is a highlight of my week. I start going to the gym at least once a week too. It's a fairly ordinary exercise routine, but it helps.

I think about creating a physical training program for corporate people who spend their whole day sitting at a desk—something to deal with their mental stress as well as the punishment to their bodies. *Maybe I could make a program and test it out on the Megaport staff?* Anything would be better than making another sales call. But I force myself to stop daydreaming and pick up the phone, because I'm not a personal trainer, I'm a sales rep.

I feel a terrible pressure to be successful in this role, because Bevan has been so generous, but I just can't see how it's going to happen. And what's worse is that everyone in the office knows I got this job because of who I am, not what I can do. They know that Bevan hired me as an Olympic champion, a gold medal winner, and I think they expect me to be a confident and effective person who wins at everything, including selling a niche technology. When they find out I'm not, I'm scared they'll think I'm some kind of fraud.

As bad as the job is, it turns out I have nothing to worry about with my colleagues. They're such lovely people. Such epic nerds—but it turns out that nerds are my people:

hilarious and self-deprecating, and always clowning around. They teach me the office life essentials, which is basically how to send memes and funny gifs to my workmates. And when I'm not wriggling around in my seat and watching the clock, that's what I spend much of my time doing.

After just three months at Megaport I know I need to quit. In that time, I do manage to set up a few meetings, but they don't go well. I'm self-conscious anyway, but when the clients recognise me things are that much worse. I know that I'm in over my head, having meetings with people who are experts in their field, and they have an expectation that I am a competent person. They're smiling at me, waiting to be dazzled by my Olympic-level abilities, and I am cripplingly aware that I am about to let them down. Then I do let them down, and it's horribly awkward. They're very, very nice about it—because I'm Libby Trickett—but that only makes it worse.

I spend a lot of time at work crying in the toilet, feeling totally overwhelmed. I have never failed like this before. I had my moments when I was swimming, but that didn't feel so pathetic. At that level of sport, even when you're failing you're still one of the best in the world. Now I was failing at normal life! So many people go to work in an office every single day and they're good at it, and yet I am terrible. *Why is this so hard for me?*

I have a fierce sense of loyalty, which adds to the problem. Bevan has gone out on a limb for me and I feel an overwhelming sense of guilt and shame that I have disappointed him. I have never stuffed up so spectacularly, and the fact that I've wasted someone else's time and money is cripplingly embarrassing. Perhaps with some training I could have become a capable sales person, but I clearly don't have what it takes to work at a tech start-up. I'm not a self-starter. I don't have the independence, or the experience. Bevan threw me in the deep end and I sank like a boulder.

I don't even want to look Bevan in the eyes, but I have to if I'm going to quit the job. And I really do have to quit the job. I need to step out of the way so that Megaport can use my salary to employ someone who actually knows what they're doing—who can help the company succeed.

Bevan and I sit down on the leather couches in the foyer of the Megaport offices, and I apologise and resign. And he is so lovely about it that he inadvertently makes me feel worse. He apologises too, and acknowledges that the circumstances haven't been ideal: he says I wasn't set up to succeed. Bevan is a mentor and a friend, and I don't think he ever had me up on a pedestal, but I wonder if he is a bit disappointed that his Olympic champion came up short. We agree that I'm not good for the job and the job isn't good for me. 'Part of learning what you do want to do is learning what you don't want to do,' Bevan tells me, wisely. 'It's got to be the right fit.'

But maybe I'm just not right, period, and I never will succeed again. I'm persevering with the television opportunities, but it feels like an awkward fit. I don't fit in an office either—that much is clear. Life has been really tricky since my swimming career ended . . . I don't seem to fit anywhere anymore.

2005

'You must do the thing you think you cannot do.'

—Eleanor Roosevelt

Whatever plagued my performance in Athens, it fell away at the 2004 World Short Course Swimming Championships in Indianapolis the following October. I had an absolutely monstrous run, winning gold in the 100-metre freestyle, my first individual gold on the world stage. I swam the fastest freestyle split in history in the 4x100-metre medley, helping the team to a world record and another gold medal. I also won a silver in the 50-metre freestyle, a bronze in the 50-metre butterfly, a bronze in the 4x100-metre freestyle, and a silver in the 4x200-metre freestyle. I was on fire.

My personal life was cooking too. At the end of 2004, after nearly two years of long-distance dating, Luke moved from Sydney to Brisbane, and into my mum's house. Our relationship had been pretty intense from the start; you have to be fairly serious about a person to even think about doing the long-distance thing. When we saw each other over those first two years, it was in intensive blocks. We'd spend a whole weekend together, or a whole week, living in each other's pockets, and we spoke to each other almost every night when we were apart. I was only nineteen when we decided to live together, but we had a very strong connection. He made me feel loved and he made me laugh, which I valued more than anything. I knew intuitively that I wanted to spend my life with someone who made my life fun.

On Valentine's Day in 2005, Luke and I went out in Sydney to celebrate our second anniversary. We had dinner at our favourite Thai place, then went home to his parents' place, donned our scummiest pyjamas and climbed into his king single bed together. This is where he decided to propose. He pulled out a ring from under his pillow, which he'd had on lay-by for more than a year, and said, 'Hey, do you want to marry me?' He was 22 years old at the time, and I was 20. I was incredibly happy.

In some ways my swimming career infantilised me because I didn't have to deal with a lot of day-to-day responsibilities. In other ways it forced me to grow up quickly. There were so many pressures and expectations attached to my career, and levels of commitment and focus that were far above what most 20-year-olds were expected to have. My life was incredibly structured and incredibly demanding, and Luke understood it. I could never have been with anyone from outside the swimming community. He had always supported and encouraged me, and that was precious to me. We fitted together. And because I was used to making big commitments, I wasn't afraid of committing to Luke.

Having said that, it was difficult living with Luke at Mum's place, which was just as tumultuous when I was in my early twenties as it had been when I was a teenager. My brother Stew was battling a lot of demons, and it was hard to balance his needs with what was now a super-elite training cycle, not to mention a live-in boyfriend.

Luke and I lasted about two months at home before we started house hunting. Fortunately, I had enough money to look at buying an apartment, because I was raking it in with sponsorship deals and occasional public appearances. I had signed on as an ambassador for Speedo just before Athens, which meant I had a steady income, and my status as the world record holder meant a lot of other sponsors came on board after that. I would go on to work with Fuji-Xerox, Telstra, Rebel Sport, BHP and Rio Tinto, Lenovo, Uncle Toby's and even KFC (not my finest hour), which gave us an unusual level of financial freedom for our age. My training regime was intense, but Stephan knew how tough things were for me at home so he supported our move. All he said was, 'You should have done it yesterday.'

As keen as we were to set up house, I quickly realised I wasn't very well prepared for the task because Mum had always taken care of me. I couldn't cook a thing, at first. I had to buy recipe magazines and teach myself, one painful meal at a time. But I soon learned not to burn tea towels, and how to cook a mean Cornish pasty. Luke couldn't cook either when we moved in together, but he wasn't too fussed about it. I tried to force him to make dinner once a week, but he'd ask me for instructions every thirty seconds. I gave up on it pretty early on—it was just faster if I did it myself, and Luke was very happy with that.

It had been such an incredible privilege living at home with Mum, and having her do everything for me so that I could just focus on training, but there was something really satisfying about doing my own laundry too. The first few times I put a load in the washing machine, I sat and watched while the clothes tumbled about. *I did that*, I thought to myself. *Aren't I a clever girl?* The novelty wore off fairly quickly, of course.

The next major international swimming meet in 2005 was the World Championships, which happen every two years. Going into that competition, I felt I had learned to deal with pressure and expectation. I had been under the microscope in Athens, and even though I didn't have the most glorious

outcomes, going through it had made me tougher and therefore a better competitor. I also thought I had a point to
prove. I knew the world hadn't seen the best of me yet.

I felt like Stephan expected more of me than the other
athletes that he trained. He knew what I was capable of and
he had huge expectations. I was under constant pressure.
He was not an easy man—not by any stretch of the imag-
ination. There was no cuddling or mollycoddling, and he
had an uncanny ability to make you feel guilty as hell. In
training, he would only have to tell me that I didn't push
hard enough on my last 50 metres and I would immediately
feel ashamed. He never yelled, but the guilt I felt made me
want to push harder and go faster. It made me want to
please him.

He was so driven, as a coach. He wanted to be a better
coach than he was a swimmer, I think. Sometimes being
the athlete isn't the thing. Having experience as an athlete
teaches you critical lessons that you bring to coaching, but
you work so much harder as a coach. That was my impres-
sion of Stephan—he excelled as a coach, and bore no
frustration or regret about what had come before. He had a
burning desire to be brilliant at his own job, which was to
make us as swimmers as good as we could be. It was other-
worldly to meet someone who was such a perfect match for
me at the exact time that we met. It's like that saying: 'When
the student is ready, the teacher will appear.' That's what it
felt like with Steph.

We had different strengths. I had the talent and the focus, but it could be a very volatile energy and I needed to be pointed in the right direction. Stephan was clinical, a perfectionist. He was a bit like a robot at times. The lack of emotion, that propensity to solve problems rather than express empathy, were traits which he shared with Luke, but are traits that are better suited for me to have in a coach. Stephan was clinical and clear. He learned very early on with me that I had intense, sometimes extreme emotions, which no doubt was frustrating for him, but he always kept a poker face when I was having a meltdown. 'I just wish you would take the emotion out of it, do the work and then perform on the day,' he once said. I don't blame him—I know I could behave like a big toddler sometimes. But I think my emotions and my passions are part of what made me a great swimmer. I think Stephan knew that too.

Going into the World Championships trials in Sydney, I knew I had to blow the competition away. Only the top two qualifiers in each race would join the Australian team in Montreal. The 100-metre freestyle was my strongest race, but Jodie Henry had eclipsed my world record in Athens and there was no telling what would happen. All the medals I had won at the World Short Course were irrelevant when we were swimming in a 50-metre pool—at least, that's how it felt. I had become absorbed into goal-oriented thinking where you're only as good as your next achievement, without savouring what you have just achieved.

I started strongly at the trials, qualifying for the 100-metre butterfly and the 50-metre freestyle. I also qualified for the 4x200-metre freestyle team, which I'd started dabbling in purely to improve the back end of my 100-metre race. Unfortunately, the 100-metre freestyle was where I let myself down. I finished third, which meant I'd missed my chance—I wouldn't be competing at the World Championships in the race in which I had recently held the world record.

The result was bitterly disappointing, made worse by the fact that I had actually swum a good race. It just happened that Alice Mills and Jodie Henry were faster than me on the day, with Alice taking the national title that year. I was so happy for Alice, who probably felt like she was forever running just behind Jodie and me.

I had a huge amount of respect for the women I competed against, which only made me feel worse about my own shortcomings. I certainly found Jodie frustrating—she was so crazy talented that it felt like things came much easier to her than they did to me. In my mind, it felt like she did less work but was able to achieve such incredible things, and was always so laidback. Alice, on the other hand, had my intense focus but worked even harder than me. I felt awed by both of them.

We weren't really encouraged to be friends when we were competing; if we had been, we may have found that we actually had a lot in common. It wasn't until later in life that we forged deeper connections. As young women, we were kind to each other and we made each other laugh, but we kept our distance, psychologically and emotionally, probably with some influence from our coaches. And it would likely have been difficult to compete at that level if I cared too much about my rivals. But I cared enough, and I empathised enough, to want to celebrate Alice's win. I was genuinely happy she would get her day in the sun, but I was devastated that I had missed an individual spot in the 100-metre freestyle at the World Champs.

To make everything worse, after the race Channel 9 asked me to join Alice and Jodie in for their interview. 'Why? I came third,' I said, annoyed, but they insisted. They were just playing up the drama of an unexpected upset. It detracted from Alice's moment, and it put me in the spotlight when all I wanted to do was run to the change rooms, climb into the shower and cry.

After trials, my goals for the World Championships shifted. Stephan and I decided that the best path forward was to try to make the 4x100-metre medley team, even though I wasn't the fastest qualifier in any of the strokes. The idea was that I would put in such a monster performance in the 4x100-metre freestyle, which was earlier in the program, that I would make it impossible for the coach of the medley team not to select me for the freestyle leg of that race.

Usually it's a given that the person swimming the individual 100-metre race would take that spot—which for the freestyle leg would be either Jodie or Alice. But Jodie, Alice and I were all in the same league. We weren't just the top three female freestyle sprinters in Australia, we were the top three in the world, so it wasn't completely delusional to think that I could deliver a performance in the earlier 4x100-metre freestyle relay that made me the best choice for the medley relay later in the week. The medley team was selected based on form. It didn't matter if you had an amazing run at trials—if you weren't performing under competition conditions, someone else would get the spot.

I had to prove myself in every race I swam, and I did just that in Montreal. I took a silver medal in the 100-metre butterfly and did a personal best time, finishing just behind Jess Schipper. It was amazing having Australians come in first and second, and it meant I got to sing the national anthem on the podium even though I didn't actually win. We also won gold and broke a Commonwealth record in the 4x100-metre freestyle, which was deeply satisfying for me on many levels, because I always seemed to have something to prove.

Before the final of the 4x100-metre freestyle relay, I approached the coach of the medley and freestyle relay teams, Shannon Rollason, and asked to lead off so I could get an accurate and official time for my leg of the race. The other legs of a relay are all 'flying starts' over the head of the girl who has just swum; the split time is between one girl touching the wall and the next girl leaving the blocks, which means the timing of the lead leg and the subsequent legs is not strictly comparable. Shannon, who was also Alice and Jodie's coach, denied my request. I think he was probably conscious that I would be trying to qualify for a spot on the medley team, but it was just as likely that he said no simply because I'd had the cheek to ask. There was no love lost between Shannon and me. I was always fastest off the block—that was my strength—but he was unfazed. He told me that just after the Olympics was a good year to change things up and see how a different combination worked, and proposed that I anchor the team instead.

Again, I was devastated. *How can I possibly make an argument that I should be selected for the medley relay when I won't have a clear time?* Part of the problem was that I had almost assumed I would get the first leg of the freestyle relay. I was blindsided by my own optimism. I felt so frustrated and powerless that at first all I could do was cry hot, angry tears in my hotel room. But eventually I calmed down and decided that I had to make the best of the situation. If I had to swim a truly extraordinary leg in the freestyle relay that left no doubt about my speed, so be it. I couldn't let it shake me—I had a job to do.

Jodie led off in the freestyle relay, Alice was second, Shayne Reese was third and I brought us home. Jodie swam her leg in 54.4 seconds from a flat start, and Alice did hers in 53.9 seconds. I saw Jodie's time as I was waiting to swim and knew I had a chance of beating it. It was a flash of a thought, gone almost instantly. Then my mind went blank, I hit the water and my race came together beautifully. I had a fiercely held goal, but I let it go when I had to and let my body take over. And I swam my leg in 53.5 seconds, almost a full second faster than Jodie.

It was exactly what I wanted—a clear indication that I was in great form. I felt good, my body felt good, the taper had gone well and my race process was bang on where I wanted it to be. That mental aptitude for competition had served me well. I didn't have to deal with the level of scrutiny at the World Championships that I had experienced in Athens—we were being broadcast but it didn't feel like the eyes of the entire world were on me—and I felt much stronger mentally as a result. I focused on what I could control and let go of the things I couldn't, including the fact that Jodie and Alice still had to swim the individual 100-metre freestyle race. If Jodie or Alice pulled out a 53.7 or better, my chance of swimming the medley was gone, so it was completely out of my hands.

I swam the 4x200-metre freestyle race the same day that Jodie and Alice swam their heats for the 100-metre freestyle. It kept my mind occupied and kept me in the water—as I saw it, any chance to race was a chance to get more competition experience and stay match-fit. I also just loved racing. I smashed the first leg of the race, and surprised even myself by breaking the Commonwealth record for the 200-metre freestyle, and our team won the silver medal. Meanwhile, Jodie won the 100-metre freestyle in 54.18 seconds. Her time wasn't extraordinary—they rarely are for any swimmer the year after an Olympics—but she won the World Championship; in terms of staking a claim for the medley race, she had done a damn good job. I had also done everything within my power, and now it was out of my hands. As much as I wanted that spot on the team—and I was ravenous for it—I felt satisfied that I had given it my best shot. No regrets.

The following day, the day of the 4x100-metre medley heats, Shannon told me I'd done it—I was on the team. The decision must have been tough, but with the times and the results we'd all swum, I think it was fair. I did feel bad for Jodie and Alice, but for myself I was elated. I had made good on a modified goal. I had adapted to disappointment and come out fighting, and in the race I did both Shannon and Stephan proud. I absolutely smashed it—I swam my leg in 53.1 seconds. Alongside Jess Schipper, Leisel Jones and Sophie Edington, we won gold in the 4x100-metre medley final and set a new Commonwealth record.

I won gold in the 50-metre freestyle as well—my first individual gold medal at a major championships. This was the point where I felt like my swimming career was really starting to take off. I was getting better. My form was getting better and I was getting more consistency in my performance. But I also had a growing mental toughness that gave me an edge. I was extremely proud of myself for adapting to the disappointment—for absorbing it, refocusing my mind and moving forward. To come away with three gold and two silver medals was a massive feat, and I felt my confidence become that much stronger. *Good, I can do that,* I thought to myself. *Now, what am I going to do next?*

Chapter Five

2014

'Every experience, no matter how bad it seems,
holds within it a blessing of some kind.
The goal is to find it.'

—Buddha

I have naturally elevated levels of testosterone, which I guess is part of the reason I did so well in my swimming career. I'm stronger than other women and I can recover faster, but the testosterone wreaks havoc with my menstrual cycle. I didn't really notice it as a teenager, and I was on the pill the whole time I was training, but since I came off it my cycles have been all over the place—sometimes 30 days long, sometimes 60. I've been diagnosed with polycystic ovarian syndrome (PCOS) and they tell me getting pregnant could be difficult, but it's okay—I'm up for the challenge.

Getting pregnant is my next goal, and after Megaport I really need something major to focus on, something meatier than a five-minute breakfast TV slot and the massage and personal training diplomas I'm only half-heartedly committed to. Having a baby feels like a solid choice. Luke's finance business is growing, slowly. It's time to start the next chapter of our lives.

Irregular cycles make it really hard to know when I'm likely to ovulate. It could happen any time across a span of three or four weeks, and I have to look for signs that it is happening, which means I'm suddenly hyper-aware of my reproductive system. I have to count calendar days and worry about things like my basal body temperature, cervical mucus, twinges on my uterus that might signal implantation and then vague pregnancy symptoms. I have to map, and study, and think about the plan. I have to work towards the goal.

I don't have lengthy conversations with Luke about cervical mucus. He's only vaguely aware of what PCOS is, and he's very happy to let me manage the details. I think he figures that I'm the best person to oversee what's going on inside my body; his job is to front up and do the deed every second day, like a good husband. Rain, hail or shine, he is expected to perform, even if he's busy, if he's running late, if he's tired. I love my husband very much and he's a total spunk, but this routine is not exactly romantic. It's not *sexy* and it's not *fun*. We're very committed to the job, however, and boy, are we good at it. Practice makes perfect. It feels like a lot of effort and a lot of concentration on my part, but it pays off relatively quickly in the end. We kick off in May and the first cycle is a non-starter, but by mid-July I find out that I'm pregnant.

Pregnant in the second cycle! Early triumph! I feel all the normal giddy feelings you get with this news, plus a little something extra—something like relief. I thought it would be hard and it really wasn't at all, and this seems especially awesome to me. It gives me an extra bounce in my step. Luke, ever the moderate guy, is very happy that we're pregnant but doesn't quite get my sense of triumph. He wasn't anxious about the PCOS situation so he doesn't share that special feeling that we beat the odds. This stuff is all in my head.

I feel incredibly motivated all of a sudden. I have a clear purpose in life that is every bit as important as training for a gold medal, and that's how I try to approach it. At the beginning of a training cycle, I would sit down with my coach and talk about my goals, and we would develop a plan to achieve those goals. My goal now is to have a baby, and I have already put the program into place. The pregnancy was the first milestone; now I have appointments to make, a home to prepare, a name to choose, all that stuff. None of this is urgent but it feels good to have something meaningful to focus on. God, how I've missed that feeling.

It's unclear exactly how far along I am because of my irregular cycle, so my GP sends me for an early scan to figure it out. 'Roughly seven weeks,' the sonographer tells me. 'There's your baby's heartbeat.' On the monitor, I see a tiny, flickering pulse in the middle of a tiny little bean, and I feel a rush of absolute joy. *There you are, bunny! Already on your way.* Unbelievable. It just feels *unbelievable*.

At home, I jump online and start searching for statistics around seeing a heartbeat at seven weeks. I'm absolutely positive that this is a great sign for the pregnancy, and I want the internet to agree with me. It does—the baby is growing strong. A tough little bean, like Mum.

I feel such a strong connection to this little human, who is just barely there. This baby is already a person to me. I can't stop thinking about that little heartbeat, pummelling away. I wonder what gender they will be. I wonder what they will be like, what their life will be like, who they will grow up to be. My excitement is not really about having a baby—I'm actually not much of a baby person, to be honest—it's about the whole journey ahead. I'm just so keen to meet my child and see who they become.

I find it so bizarre that this baby is a physical part of me and Luke—they will grow into a wholly unique individual, and be an adult one day. And I get to experience and influence that adult taking shape. I'm excited to share the things I love with my child, and to learn about the things they love. I wonder if they'll have some spark of creativity, which Luke and I completely missed. Will they sing? Will they dance? Will they play an instrument? Will they be academic, like their dad? Or will they swim, like me? I wonder who they'll look like—me or Luke? They say the baby always looks like its father when it's born, but I'm convinced that we'll have a blond baby, although I have no idea why.

My baby is such a lovely thing to think about, and I think about it and think about it, all day long. There are so many daydreams in my head.

I've been looking at this pregnancy as a life goal, but this goal feels so big and bright and happy that it's not like my swimming goals at all. The competitiveness is gone. The punishment, the hard work, the sacrifice. I'm on a journey and there is somewhere I want to get to, but the pregnancy is a far lighter burden. In some ways, I know, it's because I feel like being pregnant is 'ordinary'. Of course, this is the most important thing that has ever happened to me and Luke, but the rest of the world doesn't care. I won't have the eyes of the world on me when I'm giving birth (thank god). And it's nice to feel like I'm doing something worthwhile when there's no pressure for me to be the best. I don't have to win this time around, I just have to cross the finish line.

Some women opt for experience, but I decide I want a younger obstetrician. Male or female doesn't bother me, but I want someone with a bit of energy. My GP recommends a specialist named Dr Rob Butler, so I hop online to do my research and it's obvious that this is my guy. He's a former athlete, for one thing. Before becoming an obstetrician, Rob was an elite rower and he still competes in triathlons. He's also very handsome, which doesn't hurt. My very own McDreamy. *Ticks all the boxes!* I smile.

Our first appointment with Rob is around the nine-week mark, and he ushers us into his office in South Brisbane with a warm smile on his face, which puts Luke and me at ease instantly. The banter is great, light-hearted and familiar, so I know I've picked a winner. We talk weather, sports, work, the usual nonsense, and then he asks us about our baby.

'Nine weeks, you reckon,' Rob says. 'Right, let's take a look.' He takes me over to the examination chair. He tells us that he'll do a scan every time we visit, just to see how things are travelling, and I mention that we've already had a scan and that we saw the heartbeat. 'That's a great sign, right?' I say. Rob agrees.

He closes a small curtain around me so that I can take my pants off and get into position, and then we begin the very awkward process of having an internal ultrasound. I drape a cloth over my lap for modesty and assume a very neutral look while Rob rolls a big condom over the scanning probe and smothers the top of it with some kind of lubricant. This stuff is so embarrassing, but Rob is a professional. He manages somehow to insert the thing while looking the other way.

I manage to keep a straight face, I think, but it's a challenge. I'm amazed I don't start giggling.

It's funny how the air can get heavier from one moment to the next. We're all smiles, ear to ear, then the probe goes in and suddenly Rob is somewhere else. I'm still sitting there on the bed feeling goofy, but then I get the sense that I'm trailing behind, like I missed some important bit of information in a movie. The atmosphere has changed, but I don't understand why exactly. Nothing has happened but something is clearly *happening*.

Rob is very quiet. He's moving the probe around and searching the screen, looking for something, and I find myself scouring the monitor, too, because I want to help him find whatever he's looking for. The next minute drags. It feels like an hour, because I'm holding my breath.

Rob sighs. He marks two points on the image with a cursor and removes the probe, pulls the latex gloves off his hands and throws them in a small rubbish bin, pumping antibacterial gel onto his hands and rubbing them together as he speaks. 'I'm sorry,' he tells us, 'I can't find a heartbeat.'

He explains that the two points he marked on the screen indicate the size of the embryo, which likely stopped growing at around eight weeks. A missed miscarriage. For a week at least, I thought I was pregnant when the baby inside me was dead.

Rob is talking but I can't think. I'm listening and I'm not—I feel like I've been punched in the heart. I'm just sitting there with the stupid modesty cloth over me, feeling numb and disoriented, but also as though I'm going to be sick. Maybe I can throw up in that little rubbish bin. I'm trying to pay attention to the detail because I want to understand what is happening, and Rob is explaining it to me right now in this kind, but also perfunctory way. His voice is telling me something that he's not saying with words, and I'm trying to figure it out. He is gentle, but professional—maybe that was the problem. I realise that he's made this speech a hundred times before, thousands maybe, because what is happening to me is so totally ordinary. It happens every day. I feel like I'm drowning. I feel like a tidal wave is crashing over my head, but my doctor is saying, in the kindest possible way: *Miscarriages are common—this is not a tragedy.*

I haven't been around many pregnant women in my life. All the women I knew in the swimming scene were on the pill, their bodies trained for another purpose. I didn't know, or I don't remember, that one in four pregnancies ends in miscarriage. If I knew, I guess I just didn't think those odds applied to me. The odds had never applied to me. And anyway, I got pregnant fast and we saw a heartbeat, which meant we were good. We were lucky. There was nothing to worry about. I hadn't shared the news with anyone because you're not supposed to do that until the twelve-week mark . . . I didn't really consider why but now I know.

I haven't told Mum. I have to call her now and say, 'Mum, we got pregnant, but I've lost the baby.'

I was so excited to tell you.

Rob gives me the option of letting nature take its course and waiting days or weeks for my body to eject the foetus, or having a dilation and curettage operation to remove it straightaway. The athlete in me takes over immediately— I want a D&C. The sooner we reset, the sooner we can try again, get back on track. If we move forward, I can leave this pain behind, this deep cut in my chest. Besides, the idea of sitting and waiting for my baby to slip out of me is horrifying. I can't do it.

I'm due to travel to China in a few days to be a swimming commentator at the Youth Olympic Games—my first commentary gig. Before the scan, I'd asked Rob what food I should avoid while I was over there, what precautions I should take. After the scan, it's a different conversation, but I'm still determined to go.

Luke is worried, but in my infinite wisdom, my mule-like stubbornness, I decide that throwing myself back into work will mute the heartbreak. I'm going to have a D&C, and then I'm going to jump on a plane to Beijing to do something that is unfamiliar and pretty far outside of my comfort zone. The Olympic Broadcasting Services have already paid for my ticket and my hotel, and they've set a broadcast schedule, and I don't want to leave them in the lurch. I also don't want to let something else go, because it feels suddenly like my whole life is coming apart. For about five minutes, going to China strikes me as the most sensible thing to do next. It doesn't take me long to realise that I'm not thinking straight.

After the procedure, I bleed so heavily that I have to stay in hospital overnight. And for days and days afterward I bleed and have severe cramps. While my body is breaking down, my mind is following suit. This is a tailspin. I feel totally numb one minute, and then I cry uncontrollably. Of course I couldn't go to Beijing; I could barely leave the house. But I've never backed out of a commitment before and it feels really shameful to me. I feel like I've let everyone down. Luke goes back to work the next day, and I sit at home, weeping. I weep and I eat, for days and days, bingeing on garbage, trying to stuff the feelings down with food.

Things happen for a reason, I think. *What did I do? I must have done something wrong.* I retrace every step in my head, everything I ate, everything I drank, everywhere I went. Rob said these things just happen sometimes and nothing can be done to stop it. 'You didn't drink too much coffee, you didn't exercise too much, the bath water wasn't too hot. Sometimes the chromosomes in the foetus aren't right so it just stops growing.' But I can't shake the feeling that it was my fault. 'That's how many women feel after a miscarriage,' Rob says. 'But it isn't correct.'

The internet says the same thing—I've read all about it. I eat chocolate and I google and read articles and forums, and I cry. I know I'm not alone, and that some pregnancies just aren't meant to be. But I feel so alone, so ashamed and heartbroken, and so convinced that I have done this to myself.

Stephan would tell me to focus on the next thing. That's my instinct too. Some part of me just wants to put this aside, use a power phrase to clear my head, put all the confusing thoughts aside. But my heart is broken. And there's nothing else. I realise, maybe for the first time in my life, that I need to sit with the grief for a while. I need to stay home and cry when I want to cry. The only way I'm ever going to get over this pain is to go straight through the middle of it.

But I know I also need a new goal or I'm not going to get through it. That's just how I'm built. I can suffer, but I need to know there's light at the end of the tunnel—that all this darkness is going to end at some point. I'm desperate to know when we can start trying again. Rob says I have to wait a full cycle, which feels like a lifetime. All I can do is focus on preparing my body so that when the time comes, we're ready. I start watching the calendar again, because it's something to hold on to, and planning makes me feel strong. *I can get pregnant*, I think. *I will get pregnant again*. But some days it feels like I'm drowning.

*

You only hear about other people's miscarriages after you tell them about yours. Mum had a miscarriage, which I kind of knew, but we'd never really talked about it. After my oldest sister was born, Mum got pregnant and lost the baby. She was at home alone with my sister, who was a toddler at the time, and she started bleeding while she was standing at the kitchen sink. That was it. She's very stoic when she remembers it, but I can sense her sadness because the memory is still so vivid for her. I feel closer to her now than I ever have, connected by our loss.

I'm also hearing about women from the swimming community who have had not just one but multiple miscarriages. I wonder if our training has something to do with it, and feel another stab of guilt. I also feel guilty that I didn't know what these women were going through at the time—that there's a stigma around miscarriage that makes us want to be discreet. It's awful, but I understand that instinct because I don't want to broadcast my grief. I don't want people, especially mothers, to feel bad for me. I don't want people to know that I am weak, or vulnerable, or just not having a good time, because it's hard enough dealing with the grief without getting those looks of pity and concern. In my more rational moments, I know that everyone means well and that I have nothing to be ashamed of, and that if I give people a chance they'll show me the same love and support that I would offer them in the same circumstances. Even so it's difficult to shake the feeling that grief is somehow unattractive and boring. I find it hard to let people know how deeply I am hurting, so I put on a mask when I'm out in the world that looks like the old me.

A couple of weeks after my miscarriage, one of my closest girlfriends tells me she is pregnant. I want so much to celebrate with her, to be truly joyful and excited for her, because I love her. But I just can't do it. All I want is to be where she is, to have what she has, but my grief is still too close to the surface at this stage. I don't hug her as fiercely as I should. The smile on my face is wobbly and feels forced, and I find myself wanting to run away. I feel so guilty that I'm not sharing her joy as much as I know I should. She knows about the miscarriage but we haven't really spoken about it, and I won't speak to her about it now. I don't want to be a downer when she has so much to look forward to, even though it makes me feel more alone.

Why does it seem like everyone is pregnant all of a sudden? I feel like I'm surrounded. My sister-in-law is expecting her second. It feels like they sneeze and she gets knocked up. And I just found out that a couple Luke and I know, friends of friends, conceived at the same time as us. Their due date is literally the same day that our baby was due. I am truly happy for them, but the news makes my heart constrict and I have to fight back tears. It's so confronting seeing someone else living the life that I feel I should have had. Everyone else is lucky and we're unlucky. They're happy and we're not.

And it's my fault—I know it is. I'm worthless. I always have been. *I failed. Why did I fail? Why can't I get this simple thing right?* My thoughts are dark, obsessive, overwhelming. *What is wrong with my body?* I wonder. *What's wrong with me?*

2005

'Promise me you will not spend so much time
treading water and trying to keep your head
above the waves, that you forget, truly forget,
how much you have always loved to swim.'

—Tyler Knott Gregson

When I raced well, I was in the moment. I was 100 per cent present, running on autopilot, unaware of any thoughts or feelings. That's what it means to be 'in the zone'. But out of the pool, when I was thinking about my swimming career, my mind was always on the future. I was always thinking about the next step, never the here and now, which meant I never really paused to think about my achievements.

Immediately after the 2005 World Championships, I went to Duel in the Pool, an exhibition meet between Australia and the United States, and beat the recently crowned World Champion Jodie Henry in the 100-metre freestyle. I should have felt so much joy in that moment, because it was the first time I had broken through in that race. But there was barely a ripple in my head. I had started to associate satisfaction and pleasure with complacency; if I was satisfied, I wouldn't strive for more.

I wonder now if that's actually right, and whether taking a moment to stop and smell the roses isn't a better long-term strategy. I wish at least that I could remember moments like that without feeling I took them for granted. I wish I had more perspective back then. I think I would have been a better athlete. Maybe I'm wrong—maybe that singular focus and constant forward momentum is what allowed me to achieve what I did—but it often made me feel like a failure when I was at the top of the world.

If there was ever a good time for me to stop and ponder my success, it wasn't 2006. The trials for the 2006 Commonwealth Games were in January, followed by the actual games in March. Then the World Short Course Championships were straight off the back of the Games, and after all of that we had the trials for the 2007 World Championships. It was a brutal year of competition.

My goals would shift from one meet to the next. I had never been to the Commonwealth Games, so I wanted to prove myself in that arena, but above all I wanted to cement my place at the top of the leaderboard. The Duel in the

Pool was not a major championship, so I was yet to win a 100-metre freestyle event that I thought counted. I wanted to get the world record back too.

I felt like I had a point to prove with Jodie. I had always been a fierce competitor, but I'd always felt like I was competing against myself. Now I began comparing myself to the other swimmers, racing against them in my head and focusing explicitly on beating them. Jodie loomed the largest in my mind because she was my toughest competitor. I wanted to be the best, and quite often she was the only person standing in my way. This was a dangerous path. If you start thinking about your competitor, you start swimming other people's races instead of your own. This only made me more intense. Jodie was still as relaxed as ever, which only frustrated me more.

I knew that I would qualify for the Commonwealth Games—three people qualified in every race—so at the trials I was more focused on my time. I broke the world record in the 100-metre freestyle—53.42 seconds—but Stephan didn't congratulate me when I jumped out of the pool. 'Why did you do that? You went out too hard and your stroke rate was too high,' he said. He knew I was thinking about Jodie when I hit the water. 'You would have done a better time if you had swum your race properly.'

It was devastating to be chastised by him, and my body was screaming from the exertion. On the other hand, I'd swum a personal best time and broke a world record, so it wasn't at all bad news. However, I did recognise that there was a problem brewing. I was thinking too much about what was happening in other lanes—about what my competitors were doing. I also noticed that a whole lot of 'what ifs' were starting to creep into my thoughts. *What if I mistime my taper? What if someone else gets faster? What if I do badly in this race? What if my goggles break? What if I slip off the blocks? What if, what if, what if?*

I started acting out post-race interviews in my mind that were based around me losing. Before I got in the water I would imagine a journalist saying, 'You must be really disappointed,' and I would practise my response. It was like I was trying to manage the shame before it happened. *What will I say if I lose?*

I didn't think very deeply about why these negative thoughts had started to appear, though in retrospect it's obvious they were a by-product of my sharpening ambition. The higher I climbed, the more intense and impressive the goals, the greater the risk of failure. I really didn't want to fail. It created a kind of psychological instability—but as an elite athlete, I wasn't trained to explore where those negative thoughts were coming from, I was trained to still my mind. I worked with a sports psychologist but our objective was never to explore any mental-health issues I was having—it was all about peak performance. I was trained to push negative thoughts aside, though I tried to do it in a way that was positive.

When the Commonwealth Games came around in March, I flew to Melbourne with a new and improved power phrase. It started the same way: *I'm strong, I'm fit, I'm healthy, therefore I'm fast.* I added a second part to silence the anxiety in my head: *No doubts, no regrets, I'm just here to have fun.* It worked, because on some level I believed it.

With my new power phrase, the rest of the world fell away. When I swam at the Commonwealth Games, I felt the curtains drop over my lane and block everything else out. I stopped worrying about Jodie and anyone else in the pool, and just focused on my race process. And I swam like a demon. I won gold in the 50-metre freestyle, the 4x100-metre freestyle, the 4x200-metre freestyle and the 4x100-metre medley relays. I took silver in the 200-metre freestyle and the 100-metre butterfly. I beat Jodie for gold in the 100-metre freestyle, finally breaking through in that event on the international stage.

I wish I could say everything went according to plan, but it didn't. I was drug-tested at the Commonwealth Games virtually every day, because I pulled medals every day. Drug cheats are constantly improving their systems of cheating, and at the Games the process had become pretty invasive to try to combat it: we had to drop our pants, hike our shirts up to our chests and do a little spin for the inspector to prove that we weren't peeing stolen urine out of a concealed bag. I found it embarrassing but I wasn't worried about it. It was just part and parcel of the job. Besides, I knew I wasn't one of the cheats.

Shortly after the Commonwealth Games, I was notified that one of my samples had shown an amount of testosterone above the levels allowed at the event. I was in the middle of training for the World Short Course Championships and was due to leave for Shanghai in a few days. The news totally threw me out of whack. It also came in the wake of a number of media reports about me and Leisel Jones being particularly muscular at the Games. After a number of years training at an elite level, my body was changing. I was also 21 years old, so I was becoming a woman who was strong rather than a child who was strong. My shoulders were broad and my lats were well defined—my upper-body strength overall was exceptional. But my body shape was natural, or the natural result of a punishing amount of physical work, and it was hurtful to hear people speculating about it—they compared us to the Chinese drug cheats. Then the test results came in and I was absolutely floored. I felt like my core moral values were under suspicion, and I had no idea how to defend myself.

Luke and I went to Stephan's house for the very first time to try to figure out what we were going to do. He lived in a modest place in Murarrie, which felt quite dark inside, though it may have just been my mood. We didn't go any further than the front living room, where I sat on Stephan's couch feeling utterly overwhelmed. Luke and Stephan talked through the strategy—who we could talk to, what the results meant, how we could prove them wrong. Having the two most important men in my life take charge of the situation, applying their similarly analytical brains to a problem that I couldn't solve, was such a relief. I knew that Luke loved me, and in that moment I felt like Stephan genuinely cared about me, not just as an athlete but as a friend. I felt safe with these men on my side.

I didn't know at the time that the Commonwealth Games allowed for a smaller range of 'normal' testosterone readings than other competitions. Stephan figured this out pretty quickly and leapt to my defence, working fast to keep it out of the papers. I was so grateful that he took charge because I was an emotional wreck; I don't think I could have done that myself. Ultimately, Stephan was able to demonstrate that my testosterone levels had been consistent in every drug test I'd had since I was fifteen years old. For me, this was a revelation and explained so much. I had always known I was strong—now I knew why.

Unfortunately, getting the all-clear from the drug-testing committee didn't stop the growing sense of unworthiness I felt, a little seed of shame, even though I knew I hadn't done anything wrong. My record was clean and the story never made it to the media, but still I had the lingering sense that there were nameless, faceless people out there who thought I was a cheat, and I desperately wanted their approval. I wanted the world to see me as someone worthy of love.

And all I could think to do to prove myself was to keep winning races.

I delivered at the World Short Course Championships in April 2006, taking six medals home. I blitzed the 50-metre and 100-metre freestyle events, and the 100-metre butter-fly. With my team, we won gold in the 4x100-metre medley and silver in the 4x100-metre freestyle. When I stepped up to the block for the 4x200-metre freestyle, I was more nervous than I had ever been—I was so pumped I was almost shaking. *No doubts, no regrets, I'm just here to have fun*, but we were trailing when I dived into the water. In the final leg of the race, I swam over the Chinese leader. I touched the wall just ahead of her on the very last stroke, carrying our team to a gold medal. All my training and racing was starting to develop a strength I had never had before: a strong back end. This win was one of my proudest achievements, and the relay team was one of the best I had ever been part of.

Luke and I announced our engagement after I got back from Shanghai. We told the media because I had a public profile and that's just what people like me seemed to do. It was certainly what my management advised me to do. None of my friends or family had been through anything similar, so I couldn't ask them for advice, and I think as a 21-year-old

I was naive enough to imagine that the media was pretty harmless. We sold the story of our engagement to *New Idea* for $10,000 and they ran a fairly innocuous feature, with happy snaps of me and Luke in a posh hotel, grinning lovingly at each other. They had Luke give me a piggyback ride, which felt pretty silly—but what did I know? Afterwards, they offered us $20,000 for the exclusive rights to publish our wedding photos. We signed on the dotted line because, again, I just thought that's what I was expected to do. Given the nature of the day, though, we decided to donate the money to charity.

The rest of the year was a slog, and no one did particularly well at the World Championship trials in December. Four major meets in one year was a grind. By the end of 2006 I was utterly exhausted, and suddenly we had a wedding to organise. Luke and I told Stephan we wanted to get married in 2007, and asked him when he could build a break into my training schedule. He looked at the calendar and pointed to a single free weekend immediately following the 2007 Duel in the Pool. 'Here,' he said, so that was the date.

I'm not someone who cares at all about weddings, and I had enough on my plate with training, so we hired a wedding planner and Luke managed the rest. I made sure my wedding dress was nice but I didn't care how the cutlery was set or what flower arrangements were on the table. I don't really even like flowers—I'm hypersensitive to the smell. I'll take chocolates over flowers any day. My major contribution to the wedding was planning the honeymoon, which I did practically before we did anything else.

Luke had assumed we would invite my father to the wedding, so he was mildly shocked when I told him that I didn't want him to come. I didn't want the complication, and I didn't see why I should feel obliged to invite my dad when we didn't really know each other. I almost never saw him, and I never spoke to him on the phone. He hadn't been there to give me advice through any of the challenging times, and it's not like I would turn to him for advice now. There was a huge part of me that wanted him to be there, of course, the same part of me that wanted a relationship with my father that was simple and uncomplicated. But that's not the relationship we had. There was too much history, too many bad choices. I wanted Mum and I to be able to enjoy my wedding day without feeling awkward that Dad was there.

I asked my father to meet me at a cafe on James Street. I wanted to let him know in person that I wouldn't be inviting him to the wedding, and as much as I could, I wanted to explain why. I was apprehensive but I pushed my feelings aside, ignoring the depth of the hurt I felt around this issue so I could get the job done. When we arrived, we had drinks and nibbles and made light conversation, until finally I steeled myself and told him why I was there. 'Luke and I are getting married,' I said. 'But I'm not going to invite you to the wedding. This has been a very difficult decision for me.

I don't want to hurt you, but I just don't feel comfortable for you to be there on my wedding day when you haven't really been there for the rest of my life.'

I knew he wouldn't take it well. I was rejecting him, and no one likes rejection, but my dad has always had an incredible poker face. If my words hurt him, he gave nothing away. He paused for a moment and said, 'Okay.' No further comment, no questions.

I think I had imagined we might talk it over some more, and that it might even open up a bigger conversation, one I'd probably always wanted to have with him. But that was all he gave me. Honestly, I don't think I should have been surprised.

Summer flashed by, and by March I was back in Melbourne, at the 2007 World Championships. I won five gold medals that year, one for almost every race I competed in. I broke three World Championship records as an individual, and another with the 4x100-metre freestyle team. It felt like I was on fire in the pool, at the top of my game, and I carried my winning streak from the World Championships straight into the Duel in the Pool in Sydney.

The organisers had introduced a new race at the exhibition meet, a mixed-gender 4x100-metre freestyle relay with two guys and two girls on each team. Michael Phelps, who was at the peak of his career at that stage, was leading off for the American team. I was leading off for Australia. I gave him a little trash talking in the marshalling area: 'You gonna bring it? You got nothing, Michael.' It was meant to be funny—there was absolutely no doubt that the reigning male champion of the sport was going to thrash me completely—but he didn't crack a smile. Maybe he was trying to psych me out, or maybe he just didn't get my sense of humour. I was unfazed, anyway, because the Duel in the Pool was a light-hearted event. You didn't win anything but bragging rights.

I felt nothing but ease when I stepped up to the block, heard the gun and launched myself into the water. When I got to the 35-metre mark, I saw Michael's feet out in front of me and smiled internally. *Cool*, I thought, *this is going well*. Going into my tumble turn, I saw that he had already pushed off and was heading in the other direction. *Cool cool coooool*. All I could do was try to hold on and not leave my teammates with too big a gap to make up. I just dug in and kept at it until I touched the wall.

And then I turned around and saw my time—52.99 seconds. A massive grin broke out on my face, and I was suddenly elated. I was the first women in history to swim the 100-metre freestyle in under 53 seconds.

Unfortunately, because a mixed-gender relay wasn't considered by FINA as an official event, the time wasn't ratified and wouldn't be recognised. I didn't know this when I was in the pool, waving at Luke and pointing at the leaderboard proudly, but Stephan delivered the news a couple of days later. He was almost as disappointed as I was. I felt thoroughly ripped off.

To make matters a whole lot worse, there was a debate in the media about whether or not the time should be recognised, and a number of people decided I had essentially cheated. Their theory was that I only swam that fast because I was dragging off Michael Phelps. The idea was that I was swimming just ahead of Michael's wake, which gave me an extra millisecond of speed as it pushed out behind me. From 25 to 35 metres, I definitely felt like I was in a sweet spot, but the minute he pulled away from me at the wall, I fell behind his wake and it was visibly smashing me in the face.

Once again, I felt like my character was under attack—but unlike the previous year with the drug test, this time it was happening in public. It felt like everybody had an opinion, and the seed of shame within me grew a little more, though I was barely conscious of it. I was angry, and more determined than ever to prove something about myself to the world, because, in some small, dark part of my soul, I didn't feel like the world had accepted me.

Luke and I were supposed to get married at an open-air auditorium at Taronga Zoo in Sydney, but it was forecast to pour on our wedding day. There was also some concern about a possible paparazzi problem. Having paid for exclusive rights to my wedding day story, the people at *New Idea* wanted us to get married at a secure venue where I couldn't be snapped by rival publications. Per our contract, we had to protect the secrecy and confidentiality of the event. They were particularly—and weirdly—concerned about my dress.

The alternative venue we found was in Chowder Bay, a kind of wooden box that looked over the water, which reminded me of an old schoolhouse. There were views of the water from its tiny windows and it was beautifully decorated, but it was also brutally hot inside. Everyone was sweating profusely. I had to get ready in a room out the back of the sweaty wooden box because, again, the magazine was worried that I might be photographed by paparazzi if I travelled from one venue to another. I had never had a problem with paparazzi before, so it all seemed a bit ridiculous to me, but we got swept up in the paranoid demands of the magazine. Luke and I had made our bed and had to sleep in it, though it was increasingly uncomfortable.

The worst and most embarrassing security measure the magazine insisted on was the tent. On the day of the wedding, we had to enter and leave the venue via a marquee, which even had sides to prevent the three news helicopters overhead from getting any footage of my dress. I was absolutely stunned to hear the choppers overhead, but not as surprised as I was when I looked out of my dressing-room window and saw a scuba diver clamber onto the pier outside the venue, pull a camera out of his bag and point it in my direction.

There were so many things about the day that made me smile. My mother walking me down the aisle. Luke, so handsome there at the end of the aisle that it made my heart burst. Our family and friends, laughing and smiling and hugging me every time I turned around. So much of it was absolute joy.

My dad wasn't there, but Stephan came, and I had such fondness and affection for him. I cared deeply for him, but more than anything else he had my respect. He'd been there for me from the beginning of my adult life, through all the twists and turns, and I was so grateful that he was there to share this special moment with Luke and me—especially as it was his own 40th birthday! He came to see us in the dressing room before the reception, congratulated us and told me I looked beautiful. For maybe the first time in our relationship he seemed full of open kindness and love. It made me smile. I didn't need Stephan to be kind to me in the pool, but he was still one of the most important men in my life. He was definitely a father figure to me—the only one I ever really had.

At the end of the ceremony, we were hustled through the tent and into a limousine with blacked-out windows, which drove us back to a reception room at Taronga Zoo. The room had a beautiful view but we couldn't see it—the curtains had to stay closed throughout the reception. From our guests' perspective, the day went really well. They had quite an adventure, being secreted down in buses to the venue in Chowder Bay and then back to the zoo for the reception. They got to hold some animals—an echidna, a koala and a crocodile. They also got to go outside and see the view. It was only me who was trapped inside, hiding from the media storm I'd created.

This was certainly not what I had expected, nor what I wanted for my wedding day, but the reality was that I had allowed it to happen because I hadn't had the strength to say, 'No, that's not going to work for me.' I regret signing up with the magazine—though it did give me the opportunity to support three special charities—and I regret being rail-roaded after the fact by people who clearly didn't care about my feelings.

What I regret most of all is that we didn't organise our own wedding photographer. We just figured the *New Idea* photographer would capture everything. But their photo-grapher was on a job, and he wasn't working for us. He didn't care about our memories, or our family and friends, just the kind of insincere close-up shots of the bride and groom that look good in a glossy magazine. We didn't get a group shot of the guests, or any family photos. We didn't get pictures with the beautiful harbour behind us, even though it was glistening after the rain. I can see it in my mind's eye, but that's the only place I'll ever see it. *New Idea* sent us a bunch of images from the day, but I have never printed any of them out.

The worst part of the whole experience was the nastiness that it seemed to trigger in the Australian press. It felt like rival media outlets had decided to cut me down to size in retaliation for not getting the exclusive story—if they couldn't run a picture of my wedding dress, they'd run an article shaming me for hiding it. The *Daily Telegraph* ran a particularly brutal piece the following day, just as we were leaving for our honeymoon, saying I had allowed my wedding 'to be hijacked'. The maliciousness made my head spin.

Lizard Island, in the middle of the Great Barrier Reef, is one of the most pristine, spectacular places I have ever been. We went there for our honeymoon and sank right in for five days. It was expensive to book but once we got there everything was included, and we made the most of it. Breakfast was included, so we ate breakfast twice every day. We had dinner on the shore and went ocean fishing; we took a dinghy to a secluded beach and had a romantic picnic. We swam in the crystal-clear waters, snorkelling above the most beautiful fish, turtles and coral.

It was enough to make me stop thinking, just for a second, about everything that had gone wrong over that year. The failed drug test was gone, the frustration over the world record was gone, the wedding blues were gone. I forgave myself for a lot of things, just for a second, and allowed myself to just be happy with the man I loved. It was beautiful. But I came crashing back down to earth before we even left the island.

On the morning we checked out, the hotel manager told me a letter had arrived for me and handed me an envelope. *How does anyone even know we're here?* I wondered. *And how random to get a letter on my honeymoon.* I opened the envelope and pulled out a long, handwritten note on beautiful stationery. The handwriting had the perfect slope of someone who had learned cursive before home computing was a thing. I knew it had come from an older person. I was curious but my heart sank as I started reading, and I quickly wished I hadn't opened it at all.

The woman who'd written the letter wanted to tell me how disappointed she was that I had sold my wedding story to *New Idea*. She had followed me through my entire career, she wrote, and all she had wanted was to see me on my happiest day in my beautiful wedding dress, but she couldn't afford to buy the magazine. One of the greatest joys in her life was that she was able to share her own wedding day with her family and friends through her wedding photographs, and she felt I had done myself and my fans a great disservice by prostituting myself in this way. I was a very selfish person, she concluded.

Part of me couldn't believe someone would take the time out of their day to sit down and write these things to me, but a far bigger part of me felt like my worst fears had been realised. I was not good and I was not liked. The world thought I was a drug cheat, a race cheat, a wedding cheat—worthless. I was cheap and nasty, and nothing I did was any good.

After our honeymoon I was supposed to join the Mare Nostrum Tour in Europe, a series of swimming meets that give Australians exposure to intensive racing under tough conditions. You travel and race, travel and race, building up your capacity to perform at an elite level without a lot of rest or preparation. The tour involves quite a bit of prize money, but it was also just fun travelling from one beautiful location to another over four or five weeks of the European summer. The problem was that I didn't feel like having fun.

When we got home from Lizard Island I slumped into a funk that I just couldn't shake. Luke couldn't talk me out of it, and Stephan couldn't coach me out of it. I started performing poorly at training, and eventually met with Stephen to tell him I needed a break. I sat in his office with tears welling in my eyes, unable to explain why. He was bewildered, but what choice did he have? It was clear that I couldn't perform in this state. I pulled out of the Mare Nostrum Tour, and for the next three months I dropped back to one training session a day and started eating mountains of chocolate—I've always been an emotional eater.

I just wanted to sit on the couch and cry. When I looked back over the past year, I felt so ashamed and small that I couldn't find the motivation to go on. I didn't see the greatest winning streak of my career—I only saw the ways in which people felt I had come up short. I saw the newspaper headlines, the suspicion, the letter. The letter was the feather on top of a pile of shit that made the whole thing fall over. In my mind, the public hated me, they doubted me, and they were laughing at me. All I wanted was for people to like me, but they didn't. Whether or not this was actually true had no bearing on how I felt.

Maybe I was just tired from the punishing training schedule, the back-to-back meets, the wedding, but I had hit a wall and I couldn't get over it. For three months I couldn't bring myself to care about swimming—certainly not in the way I needed to if I was going to be successful. That all this was happening just a year out from the Beijing Olympics was a problem. I could almost hear Stephan grinding his teeth, but it was pointless. I'd been knocked off my game. I was depleted, physically and emotionally. And when I did feel anything, I was just sad.

I didn't know that I had depression. In retrospect it's obvious, but I couldn't articulate it at the time. I had no language to talk about mental health, only elite performance. What was happening to me was clearly the accumulation of years of stress, pressure, expectation, drive, constant pushing, the instability that is caused when you train your mind to be laser-focused, and you push away any negative thoughts that distract you from your goal. Eventually, those thoughts were bound to come back. And when they did, they came in a flood.

Chapter Six

2015

'Courage, dear heart.'

—C.S. Lewis

My obstetrician wants me to rest a cycle, but the PCOS is so unpredictable that it could mean anything up to two months. I hate having to wait anyway—it's so damn frustrating—but not knowing how long the wait will last makes me totally crazy. I feel so out of control. The idea of having to get on that treadmill with Luke again is also pretty overwhelming. Sex every two days really kills the romance in a relationship.

In some ways, the miscarriage has brought us closer together. Every challenge we've had to face has helped us to grow and understand each other a little bit better, and Luke was heartbroken too. But I know it didn't hit him as hard as it has hit me. He is my life partner and he has always supported me, but there are times when he makes offhand comments that cut me to the bone.

'You just need to get over it, Lib,' he tells me one day a couple of months after it happened. He is so frustrated that we're stuck in the same place, talking about the same thing over and over again. He's made his peace with it, and he can't understand why I haven't. Maybe it's because I'm a woman, I don't know, but I really feel the need to talk about it. That's just how I process things. And even though we are now trying again, I still feel devastated. I can't believe we were pregnant and now we're not. I can't believe my body rejected the baby, and now we have to go through the process all over again. Luke just sighs and shrugs his shoulders. 'We just have to move on,' he says.

It's a difficult time for us. Men seem to want to fix things, but Luke can't fix this. I still get overwhelmed by the emotions, which come in waves. I feel completely despondent at times. I still think about the baby that I lost. And in between these bouts of grief and despair and this masochistic fixation with 'what I did wrong' and 'why I deserved it', I'm having mechanical sex every second day with my husband. My husband, who I love so deeply. My husband, who doesn't really understand what is wrong with me.

I struggle to have any perspective. It's not completely my fault—I just don't know any better at this stage. I'm simply not aware of the many women who struggle for years to conceive, who have multiple miscarriages, who never have the chance to have a child at all. Maybe I shouldn't feel so bad about an early miscarriage when so many women have much more significant and traumatic losses, but all I can see from where I'm standing right now is this thing that I have lost, which has absolutely crushed my heart. Like every wrong turn and every major disappointment in my swimming career, what has happened is incredibly disappointing to me because it's not what I expected to happen. I didn't imagine the worst, so I was completely unprepared for it, and I can't seem to shake away the shock.

Sometimes I wonder if, on some deep psychological level, failure just doesn't work for me. This is a hangover from my swimming career—I know that much. I am aware that I had success at a young age, and maybe it made me a little arrogant about what I thought I could achieve. The truth is you have to be a little arrogant to achieve at the highest level as a swimmer, because there is absolutely no way you can be the best in the world if you don't believe you deserve to be there. It's the only way you can compete at that level. But I recognise now that there are two sides to that coin: too much confidence and not enough wariness leaves you utterly exposed, because you're totally unprepared when things go wrong.

My grief over the miscarriage is acutely personal and intimate, but there are other things feeding into it that are only making it worse. I want to know that I'm on the right path, that I'm doing the right thing. I want to know that one day I will be successful at something other than swimming. Everything has been so piecemeal and ill-fitting since my swimming career ended that it feels like I'm never going be successful again. I feel like the world expects something of me and I can't deliver. Nothing is working.

I just want to be as passionate about something as I was about swimming. Being pregnant was so incredibly different, but it meant just as much to me.

Four months later. I know the symptoms now. I'm 60 days into my cycle, my breasts are sore and swollen, and I'm confident enough to buy a home pregnancy test. I try not to expect anything, try not to hope, but those three minutes of waiting, watching the timer on my phone, are filled with nervous anticipation. When the word 'pregnant' appears in the little window of the tester, my heart swells. But I don't want to be too happy—I don't want to assume that everything will be okay. I know now that there are no guarantees. I buy another six or seven home pregnancy tests that week, and every day I check to see if it is real.

I still feel joy, but I am so wary now, and sad that the experience seems much less innocent the second time around. Instead of feeling like I am on the verge of my next great adventure in life, I feel like we have only just passed the first hurdle. I want to get an early scan, but in mid-January 2015 I am only three or four weeks along. I have to wait at least until six weeks have passed. Slowly and cautiously, this time. We have to take each day as it comes.

At six weeks, there is a heartbeat, and I feel the knots in my chest loosen a couple of millimetres. There are other signs, too, that things are different this time. I start to feel nauseated very early. I see Rob again for a second scan at nine weeks, and there is still a heartbeat, and then the morning sickness goes next-level. It feels like the worst hangover of my life, every single day: from nine weeks through to eighteen weeks I am vomiting multiple times a day. My baby is definitely in there, making itself known. The world feels like it's constantly swaying. I have never felt so revolting. But I'm comforted by the morning sickness, in a way, because I know what it means. I am still pregnant. *I am still pregnant!* From eighteen weeks to 28 weeks I get some respite—I stop vomiting at least—but we're far enough along now for the knots to loosen a little more. At 28 weeks the nausea comes back, and it stays for the rest of the pregnancy.

The only moment of panic comes after the twenty-week scan, when the radiographer is busy measuring our baby's internal organs and checking all the fingers and toes. 'Okay, I'm just going to go and grab the doctor. He'll be back to check everything for you,' she says pleasantly, and walks calmly out of the room.

'She spent a lot of time in that one spot, didn't she?' Luke comments.

I hadn't been paying much attention. Moments later, a doctor I don't know comes in and retraces the entire scan that the radiographer has just done, pausing in the same place she did for a long while, which turns out to be the baby's liver.

'Do you see that white spot?' the doctor asks. 'It looks like calcification. It could be nothing at all, like a strawberry mole. But we need to do some more tests.'

He tells us that, at worst, it could be cystic fibrosis, but I don't really understand what that means. It's not until we visit Rob that the gravity of the situation hits me and my heart muscle clenches again. But Rob explains that both Luke and I have to be carriers of the gene and a simple blood test will tell us. It feels like I'm holding my breath for two weeks, until the test results come in. Yet again I have the feeling that things are veering off course. I still have my baby, but its future could be completely different from how I imagined. Is that something I should be sad about? I don't know.

This is the worst moment in my pregnancy, but ultimately it's a blip because I'm not a carrier. There are other tests, but the worst is over. Whatever the spot is on my baby's liver, it seems benign.

My expectations and my reality don't match up at all. I imagined that when I got pregnant, I would treat my body like a temple. I'd fuel my body with all of these amazing things and I wouldn't eat sushi or drink coffee and everything would be macrobiotic and organic and nutritious and blah blah blah. In fact, what happens is that, around week eleven, I realise that the only thing that makes me feel mildly less sick is eating KFC. Any greasy hangover food, really. I eat salty, fatty, oily food and for about an hour, I feel human. Then the fatigue, nausea and headaches come back again, and along with them comes the puking. I puke a lot.

I gain a huge amount weight, much more than the recommended guidelines, but more alarmingly I retain a massive amount of water. I swell up like a water balloon and stay that way for weeks, almost audibly sloshing when I move. It's bizarre. If I push down on my skin, particularly on my legs, the depression mark stays there for literally five minutes. It's called pitting oedema and it's totally gross—I'm like a weird water balloon monster—but I feel so violently ill that my appearance is a distant concern. I'm far more alarmed when flashing lights start appearing in front of my eyes. 'That's not good,' Rob says, running another suite of tests, then diagnosing me with gestational hypertension.

I have high blood pressure, which is a precondition for pre-eclampsia. It can be life-threatening for both the mum and the baby if eclampsia develops, but we're just monitoring things for now. With Rob's permission, Luke and I go on a 'babymoon' to Hamilton Island, one last sunny break before our lives change forever. I have the most fabulous dinner on the island one night—a gorgeous, buttery spaghetti ragu—then I waddle back to our hotel room and projectile-vomit all over the bathroom. So romantic. I develop peri-natal carpal tunnel syndrome and spend hours icing my wrists from the champagne bucket to reduce the swelling and the pain. While we're there, the pitting oedema also gets significantly worse. We call Rob and he asks us to come in immediately.

'We sort of can't—we're on an island,' I tell him.

'No problem,' he says. 'Just come in as soon as you can.'

It's Monday by the time we get back to the clinic, and in the following week there are another couple of episodes of flashing lights. On Friday, Rob sends me to hospital for observation because my blood pressure is way too high. 'It was probably high because Rob did the reading,' one of the midwives laughs. 'He gets my heart going too.' But over the weekend, Rob reluctantly decides it's time to induce. My symptoms are only going to get worse.

'I'm only 37 weeks!' I fret lamely. *The baby is coming now?* I feel ripped off that my maternity leave has suddenly evaporated into thin air. I had a whole list of television shows I was planning to watch while I was setting up the nursery. I thought I'd have another month to prepare, because first-time pregnancies are always late. I didn't want to be induced—I'd dreamed (of course) of having a natural birth while meditating and listening to whale song, but that plan seems to be out the window. On the other hand, I've been feeling so wretched for so long that having the end in sight is actually a relief.

Luke and I eat Thai takeaway before heading into the Mater Mother's Hospital on the Sunday night, where the midwives put prostaglandin gel on my cervix, which is the first step in the whole inducement process. Then, we wait. I'm swinging between fear and an incredible sense of anticipation that I'm about to meet my child. When I went to the Olympic Games for the first time I felt a similar electricity, but I didn't have this muddle of excitement and anxiety, the sense of stepping into the unknown. I have no idea what I'm doing or what to expect. I have no idea how my body will handle this process, and the risks with gestational hypertension are very real.

I start having period cramps overnight but there is no movement of the cervix, so the midwives apply another layer of gel on Monday morning. By Monday afternoon, when Rob comes to visit, I am only one centimetre dilated, but that is just enough for him to poke what looks like a little sewing hook up there and break my waters. The pain is unbelievable—truly intergalactic. It takes my breath away. I can't imagine any part of this hurting more than that.

I'm hooked up to a drip of synthetic oxytocin, which is the hormone your body releases to bring on contractions. Normally, the spread of oxytocin is slow so the contractions come on slowly, but the drip accelerates the process, from zero to a hundred in what feels like minutes. It's like dropping off the edge of a cliff. Some part of my brain is still hoping for a natural birth—as though I'm going to get some kind of prize at the end for all of my noble suffering—but that idea is quickly drowned out by the un-fucking-believable pain. After four hours of grunting and sweating, my cervix is only dilated four centimetres, which is still six centimetres away from where we need to be. 'I can't do this for another six hours,' I moan. 'Get me an epidural!'

An anaesthetist comes in to give me the spinal needle for the epidural. It's a challenging thing to do in an established labour because the contractions are so severe and I'm doubled over with the pain, struggling to stay still, but he doesn't seem to have any problems. An hour later, the pain still hasn't subsided. The contractions are coming every second minute, so it's one minute on, one minute off.

'How long should it take for the epidural to work?' I ask a nurse.

'Ten minutes,' she replies.

'Okay, it's not working.'

A second anaesthetist comes in to examine me and tells me the first guy missed my spine. Because of my scoliosis my spine curves a little, and the needle apparently went somewhere useless. The second attempt is like magic. Ten minutes, zero pain—I'm just utterly exhausted.

The team around me pauses for breath. The midwife has left the room and Rob is about to go home and grab some dinner with his family. Luke goes outside to make some calls and update our families. I'm alone in the room, enjoying this brief moment of serenity, when the foetal heart monitor suddenly drops to 40 beats per minute. The beeps slow right down, alarmingly slow, then jumps rapidly to 90 beats per minute, then drops down to 40 again. *What the hell is happening?* I draw a sharp breath and hit the buzzer for the midwife, panic rising in my throat.

She rushes in, all business, but almost as soon as she's back in the room the monitor settles back into a steady rhythm. Thankfully, Rob hasn't left yet and comes in for an assessment. 'The baby is going into foetal distress— we'll have to schedule an emergency C-section,' he tells me, hustling away to the corner of the room to organise a theatre for the surgery.

'I kind of feel like I need to poo,' I tell the nurse.

'Hmm,' she says thoughtfully. 'Let's check where you're at.' She ducks down and has a quick look. 'Yep, that baby is ready to come out.' I've gone from four centimetres to ten centimetres dilation in less than an hour, presumably because my body was finally able to relax.

'Okay, if you're ready to go, we'll go,' Rob says—so we go.

I start pushing, straining and moaning through gritted teeth. All the while, Rob is monitoring the baby very closely. It takes a full hour for the little thing to come out, and when the baby is ready Rob steps aside and invites Luke to step in and receive it. One last epic push, and out it comes. A perfect, tiny little thing.

My baby has arrived. This feeling is so big, it's hard to hold. It is so much more personal, so much less public, and so much more meaningful that any of my other achievements. But I felt prepared for those other achievements, and I'm so ill-prepared for this. It's funny to think that throughout my swimming career I spent thousands of hours in the pool, training for less than a minute of competition. You can't train for the birth experience, but it is the most protracted, physically demanding, exhausting experience my body has ever gone through. The hypno-birthing class I attended in the last trimester of my pregnancy didn't entirely work for my situation—it allowed me to go into the birth in a very positive way, but everything about meditating, my cervix opening like a lotus flower and breathing my baby down the birth canal went right out the window when the contractions started. It was a straight up hot mess.

Yet I am so proud that my body has pulled this off. I am so amazed that I've done this epic and inconceivable thing—but for some reason, I feel guilty for having the epidural. I was so sure that, as an Olympic champion, my physical abilities would mean I could have a natural birth, but it just wasn't meant to be for me. I will quickly learn that, as a mother, a constant underlying sense of guilt is unfortunately just part of the territory.

I feel a profound connection to all the other women who have been on this journey, which is a strange and beautiful feeling. But more than anything, I feel connected to Luke. I flood with love when I see our baby in his arms. This is something we have done together. And when he lays the baby on my chest and I see its perfect face for the first time, I am absolutely stunned.

Luke has missed a step, however.

'What is it, Luke?' Rob asks.

Luke forgot to check its gender. He picks the baby up again, sees the umbilical cord and proudly announces that it's a baby boy. Rob starts laughing and gently suggests that Luke check again.

'Oh, right,' Luke blushes, looking a bit more closely. 'It's a baby girl!'

I start laughing through tears of joy. 'You had one job, Luke!'

Poppy Frances Trickett was born on 31 August at 9.24 p.m. with the sweetest nose and a full head of hair. She has a small bruise on her head from the vacuum suction cup and she looks exactly like her dad, except for the curl at the top of her ears which I know so well. She has elf ears, like her mum! Even covered in vernix, with hair plastered to her head, Poppy is the most beautiful thing I have ever seen. I can't fathom how this baby can be so beautiful.

My body is pulsing with adrenaline when we meet, but the dominant feeling in my chest is not love but a sense of responsibility. She's mine and I have to protect her, for the rest of her life. *Holy crap, I created a human*, I think. I am in shock. I am in joyful but absolute shock. This thing that I have done—it's not about me, it's about her. It's feels like one of the first truly selfless things I've ever done.

Becoming a mother makes me reflect on my relationship with my own parents, and I think again about how much my mother has sacrificed for me, and wonder why my father couldn't do the same. A couple of days after Poppy is born, I include him in the group message to my closest family and friends: 'We're delighted to announce that Poppy Frances Trickett was born on the 31st of August, weighing 2.9kg and 51cm long.' My father doesn't respond at all. No phone call, no flowers, not even a text.

The rejection is like a knife. I can't tell you how painful it is that he doesn't even acknowledge my child's existence. It is one thing for him to abandon me, to reject me, but to reject my child, his granddaughter, makes me wildly angry and protective. I felt grief for her as well as for myself.

I make the decision then and there that I won't try again to include him in my life. I'm not going to bend over backwards for someone who was so seemingly fine not to have a relationship with me. It has been such an endless source of pain, and I just have to shut it down. The constant angst—*Should I try? Should I not? Why doesn't he love me? What have I done? What's wrong with me?*—I need to put it all in a box and try to move on. The scab will never heal if I keep picking at it.

2008

'Accept whatever comes to you woven in the
pattern of your destiny, for what could
more aptly fit your needs?'

—Marcus Aurelius

At 23, I was at the peak of my career. The wedding, the drug test—they were erased. After three months of grieving I had packed all my emotions about those events away and dived back into training. I was an athlete; it was etched into my cells. *Get in the water. You need to work.*

I'd won five gold medals at the 2007 World Championships, I was the reigning world champion in the 50-metre and 100-metre freestyle and the 100-metre butterfly, and I had every expectation that I would become an individual Olympic champion in Beijing in 2008, my second Olympic

Games. Four years earlier, in Athens, I had been new to the international swimming circuit—strong but green. Going into Beijing, I was an established figure in that world. Despite the tumultuous twelve months, I knew I was at the top of my game.

You never relax. That kind of success breeds high expectations—the more you win, the further you expect to go. All the dreams and goals you've been carrying around for years start to solidify until you can almost touch them. They're within reach now, but you have to focus even harder than before. I was aware that I was lucky to get a second bite at the cherry—few athletes got to compete in one Olympic Games, let alone two—and to come back even stronger, more experienced, wiser, felt like an incredible privilege. I was a champion; I could be the best in the world. I put myself under incredible pressure to deliver on that promise.

I was faster than ever, stronger than ever. My body had changed dramatically since Athens and I was proud of every sharp contour of muscle under skin. I had a lean, defined six-pack and phenomenal core strength; razor definition through my delts and lats; traps muscles like hunks of meat that you just wanted to grab and squeeze. In the lead-up to Beijing I was doing ten two-and-a-half hour sessions in the water every week, two heavy lifting sessions in the gym, pilates and yoga, and two running sessions a week. In my own time, I still did the four ab and core strengthening sessions a week, plus two half-hour sessions on a stationary bike to keep building strength and endurance in my legs. I was doing squats with 90-kilogram weights across my shoulders and chin-ups with 37 kilograms strapped around my waist. I was shredded. *Shred. Ded.*

Ironically, all I could see at the time was imperfection. As an older woman with maybe 15 kilograms of extra fat and nowhere near the same muscle definition, I am more confident and comfortable in my body than I ever was as an Olympian. At that time, my body was a means to an end, a finely tuned machine, and any sliver of weakness or imperfection was standing in the way of my dreams. I was so lean that I almost felt prepubescent—no breasts, no butt, no curve in my hips. I was fiercely proud of the control I exerted over my own body, and endlessly frustrated if it slipped out of my grasp.

Every three weeks in training we had a weigh-in and a skinfold test—a pinch test with calipers, measured down to the last millimetre. In reality, the skinfold test could vary week-to-week just because of who was conducting it, and how aggressive they were with the callipers, but if I found myself two or three millimetres over my last measurement I would walk out cursing. *What are you doing? It's not good enough!* I felt like Stephan was judging me, like the voice in my head was his, though he never said anything like the cruel things I said to myself. But if I sense some minor flicker of failure, I would double down, work harder, push myself further. And I was so tired all the time that it never really felt good. My strong body was worked so hard that it didn't feel good. But the focus itself was an addiction, a gravitational force of energy and drive that pulled me forward just as hard as I pushed myself. The intensity was incredible because the goal was incredible. I wanted to win.

When you're an athlete, you're very selfish—because you have to be. For me there was no multitasking, no real consideration of others, no compromise. The training was a sacrifice, but I did it for my own satisfaction, because I wanted to make history. And outside of training, I was lucky if I had one errand or task a day. I can't tell you how put-upon I felt having to do that one thing. I would put off going to the post office for weeks because I had to prioritise my daily two-to-three-hour nap. And if I had to sacrifice some nap time to make a sponsorship or PR-related appearance, or—god forbid—meet some family obligation, I could become genuinely frustrated, like a teenager.

I was very aware that I was one of the few lucky athletes who was fully supported by sponsorship deals, so the breakfast events, the swim clinics and the photo shoots were all part of the territory, but if they cut into my training schedule, god help somebody, at least behind the scenes. In public, I did my best to conceal how tired I was. If somebody recognised me in the shopping centre—even if I'd had a terrible day for some reason—I tried not to let on and I'd smile and sign an autograph. But my manager fielded all my business emails, so I didn't have to reply to people. I never had to say no; that was my manager's job. My job was simply to try to be the best swimmer in the world.

The Beijing trials were held at Sydney Olympic Park in March 2008. I was competing in my usual races, the 100-metre butterfly, and the 100-metre and 50-metre freestyle. I qualified for the Olympic team in the 100-metre fly on the second day of the meet, which was a huge relief. If I lost just one opportunity, one of my chances, the door would swing closed just a little and the pressure would stack on. My whole year could fall apart in a second—my whole career, if I didn't make it past that hurdle. But I knew, on day two, that I was going to the Olympics again. Everything else was cream.

My mission, my obsession, was the 100-metre freestyle. I was unofficially the first woman to swim the race in under 53 seconds, but until my time was ratified by FINA I was invisible. It was making me crazy, this idea that I'd draughted off Phelps. I knew it wasn't true and I had a point to prove.

You can never really race your competitors because you don't know what they've been doing, how well they're swimming, whether they've had a good season or been battling illness or injury. Ultimately, you're always racing yourself, and the clock. Now that I wasn't worried about making the team, what I wanted was the right time.

Winning was an afterthought; if I got the time, I would win anyway. This confidence was steady, a solid thing inside of me. I knew that if I trained my arse off, if I was physically in top form, if I was mentally focused, then I would make it bloody hard for any other woman to touch the wall ahead of me. When I stepped up to the block for the finals of the 100-metre freestyle I felt like I was soaring, an eagle. I absolutely loved that feeling.

I nailed my start off the block. I had a perfect entry into the water, had the right stroke rate and consistency. I didn't over-expend energy in the first 35 metres, I nailed my turn off the wall, and I kept just enough in reserve to smash through the last 25 metres, driving for the wall with every stroke. It sounds simple, but each element was finely tuned, practised and honed over thousands of hours. My mind was blank. My body felt perfectly balanced, running on instinct, and I knew I was ahead in the race with adjacent lead, but I wouldn't know for sure until I touched the wall and spun around to see the leaderboard—52.88 seconds. It was a tenth of a second faster than my time at the Duel in the Pool, and Michael Phelps was nowhere in sight.

The 50-metre freestyle trials came at the very end of the meet, and for me they felt like a celebration. My goal was simply to qualify for the Olympic race, and I knew that my form was good. Everything felt like it was running perfectly—I just had to deliver. I wasn't aiming for the world record because it seemed out of reach. For a long time, it had belonged to my idol, the Dutch champion Inge de Bruijn, a shredded beast of a swimmer and a really lovely woman. She had multiple Olympic gold medals and what seemed like countless world records. I just wanted to swim my best.

That meant avoiding all the things that could go wrong in a 50-metre race, which whips by so fast that it's almost impossible to swim perfectly. You have to balance a rapid stroke rate with just one breath, and be careful to balance your speed and power so you don't end up spinning your wheels. The race starts with an explosion and is over before you can even think. A lot of it comes down to luck. At the Beijing trials, luck was on my side. I can't really say how it happened, but I swam the 50 in 23.97 seconds, slashing 0.16 seconds off the world record.

I should have stopped to breathe for a moment, but I didn't. I always delayed the celebration and delayed the joy because my next goal was on the horizon. And that next goal was to win an Olympic gold medal—to step into that world and do what I set out to do.

Everything about Beijing was better than Athens for me. I was better, the trials had gone perfectly, even the Olympic Village was a better experience for me. We swam in the open air in Athens—they ran out of time (and probably money) before they could finish the roof of the stadium. We walked over dirt paths in the Olympic Village because the landscaping was just never done. Beijing, by comparison, was a model city, perfect down to the last blade of grass, with young volunteers whose only job was to rake unsightly leaves from the lawns. I ate Peking duck every day in a cafeteria the size of two football fields, while outside the Chinese government was seeding rain clouds to wash all the pollution away. Olympic volunteers stood virtually metres apart to guide us from one place to another, the smiling faces of a massive, flawless machine. The organisation was extraordinary. The hospitality was incredible. All I had to think about was the race.

My closest rivals were from the USA and Australia in the 100-metre butterfly, including Jess Schipper, who I had shadowed for almost my entire career. We both made our first youth team in 2002 and made the national team in 2003, and if anyone was going to beat me in the 100-metre butterfly, it was probably Jess. Our rivalry didn't extend beyond the pool—she was just too sweet a person. She was extremely shy, and when she wasn't swimming she was usually buried in a novel, but she had a doggedness about her that I recognised—that same hunger to be first to the wall.

I can't say we were close friends then, because we were bred to compete with each other, but there was still a genuine camaraderie between us. I was lucky that my greatest rivals in both the butterfly and freestyle were on my doorstep in Australia; they made me a better athlete. Later in life, when the competitions were over, Jess and I would become closer friends. By then we'd realised that no one but our competitors and rivals could truly understand the life we had lived. But not in Beijing.

The first day of competition was focused on the 4x100-metre freestyle relay, and the heats and semi-finals for the 100-metre butterfly. I didn't swim the heats for the relay because I wanted to conserve my energy, but I stepped in for the final and we won bronze, behind the Dutch and American teams. I couldn't help but feel the slightest sense of disappointment, because we were Olympic Champions in Athens and the World Champions the year before, but an Olympic bronze medal is still an Olympic bronze medal. And anyway, I didn't have time to think about it. I had five events to swim, with heats, semi-finals and finals for most of them, so I had to shake off the mildly disappointing start and step through my next races. You warm up, race, warm down and recover, then go back to the beginning again. It was a finely tuned process for me and required real mental discipline. *Clear your head and keep going. Bronze is still bronze.*

On day two, after a morning spent lying idly on my bunk, I came close to nirvana. My race process for the 100-metre butterfly was so perfectly synced that I felt like I was gliding through air. Everything just clicked into place. That kind of performance is difficult under the best and easiest conditions, and feels nearly impossible at the Olympic level because of the pressure-cooker environment, where you have just under a minute to prove yourself, once every four years. I swam a personal best time—56.74 seconds—and brushed up against the world record. Most importantly, I won gold. I stepped up onto the podium and the Australian national anthem played, and I smiled. I began to feel confident that it would be the first of several moments just like it over the next few days. As ever, I was immediately looking ahead. I should have stopped to breathe, to appreciate the moment, to be proud of what I'd done.

Over the next two days, I had to rest and recover, between the drug tests and the press conferences. I had regular swims to keep my body in form, to keep the fast-twitch fibres firing, but I spent my afternoons watching *Grey's Anatomy* in our village dorm room, trying to keep my mind as blank as possible. I felt relaxed and ready to roll when day five came around—the 100-metre freestyle.

When you have multiple events to swim, you try to take your foot off the accelerator during the heats and just do enough to get through to the next round. It was part of my process. I could swim the 100-metre freestyle in just under 53 seconds, but I knew I only needed to swim 54 seconds in the heats to make it through. I could conserve some of my energy for the final race by bringing it down a couple of notches, and part of the process involved trying to judge exactly how little I needed to do. No problem. I was the World Champion, but I finished fifth or sixth overall in the heats, giving me a decent spot in an outside central lane for the semi-final. I was calm, focused. On reflection, maybe I was a little too calm, too sure of myself.

In the semi-final of the 100-metre freestyle, I had a great entry, a great turn at the bottom end of the pool and just the right stroke rate. Seventy-five per cent of my race went exactly how I wanted it to—as perfect as it needed to be. I worked that first 35 metres powerfully, driving off the wall in a nice, tight somersault, pushing out in a perfect stream-line for the back half of the race. The next 25 metres felt good. I wouldn't have done anything differently. But in the last 25 metres, I took my foot off the pedal just that little bit too much—and that turned out to be a terrible mistake.

I thought there were three swimmers vying for the lead— me and two women beside me—but a fourth swimmer had pulled away in an outside lane and I didn't have her in my field of vision. So instead of gunning it in that crucial end run, I kept pace with the women beside me, then let them pull ahead slightly, thinking I would touch the wall in third. The girl in the outside lane got there first; I hadn't even seen her coming.

I touched the wall and turned to look up at the board, and in that moment saw my dreams, my work, my sacrifice, my life, imploding on a digital screen. I was *fourth*?! Fourth place in the semis was nothing. Fourth place in the semis was not going to win a gold medal; fourth place in the semis might not even get me into the final. A cavity opened up in my chest, and I felt my heart falling out. From one second to the next, all my plans, all my purpose, went up in flames. *What the hell have I done?*

I hadn't even climbed out of the pool before I started coming apart psychologically, in a way that had never happened in my entire swimming career. The more confident you are, the further you have to fall, I guess, and I was falling rapidly into the dark. My mind was racing with grief, looping and twisting and galloping out of control, a whole planet of shit on my shoulders. I was disgusted with myself for being so stupid and letting everything go. *You've done it again*, I thought. It was Athens all over again; I was doomed to repeat this stupid mistake. *You're a loser. You're pathetic. You are worthless.*

Moments after the race had ended, all my calm, all my focus, all my careful preparation was erased and I was flooded with self-hatred. My breathing was too sharp and my pulse rate was elevated, and I felt like I had no control. It was the beginning of a panic attack, which accelerated as the second semi-final came in. I waited in a corner at the end of the pool and watched, and saw with horror as my name was pushed down into ninth place. I had missed the final. Again.

You're a loser. You're pathetic. You are worthless. I was so horribly down on myself. I actively avoided eye contact with Stephan. I desperately wanted to avoid the media pool as well. By now my panic had morphed into rage and I didn't

179

think I had it in me to speak to the press, but I didn't have a choice about it because the media scrum was blocking the exit. I managed to dodge around the foreign media, but the Australian contingent was waiting for me and there was no getting around them. What could I say? What on earth was I going to say to them? *I've thrown it all away.*

I was inches away from the waiting cameras when the Australian media liaison officer stepped in front of me. 'One of the Chinese swimmers has been disqualified,' he whispered. 'You've made it into the finals.'

I didn't believe him at first—it seemed like a bizarre prank. For some reason I thought he was being cruel, trying to provoke a reaction from me. But I glanced up at the board and saw it was true. My stomach lurched again. The Chinese swimmer Pang Jiaying had had a false start and was out, and I had moved up into the final. I was sick with joy, with guilt, with shame, all at the same time. The universe had given me a second chance, but only by taking it away from another swimmer.

It didn't matter that I was in the finals. I was in freefall, and I couldn't grab hold of anything. I was still so angry at myself. All those years and months of training—all the discipline and hard work—disintegrated under the force of my self-doubt. I was four years older than I'd been at Athens, and supposedly four years wiser. I was a World Champion in the race and a world record holder multiple times over, and yet somehow I had still fucked everything up. I didn't deserve any of it. *You will never win gold in this race.* That was the dark thought driving up through the storm in my head.

Stephan met me in the corridor outside the changing rooms, looking truly shocked. 'What did you do?' he said. That was all. He couldn't possibly have said anything worse. *What did you do?* It was the unguarded shock in his voice that hurt, like he had finally seen me for the loser I was and not the champion he imagined me to be.

I was insanely disappointed in myself, because no one, not even Stephan, had higher expectations for what I should achieve than me. When it came to swimming, I was a perfectionist. I wanted to be the best, and I didn't just want to be the best for me. I wanted to show everyone what an incredible coach Stephan was, how wonderfully supportive my family was, how loving Luke was. I had failed not just myself but all of them. This is what he was saying to me. It didn't come from a place of not caring—it came from caring too much—but it felt brutal. I just wanted him to be proud of me.

Back at the athletes' village, I tried to relax. I tried to step through the process, but it just wouldn't come. Instead, I started listening to a song called 'It's Not My Time' by 3 Doors Down, which for some reason had been my pump-up song before I raced. The song had felt really positive to me before that moment. It was fierce and defiant, with lyrics that were about surviving against the odds, but it was the energy of the song that really worked for me. After that misery of a semi-final race, though, I heard the song completely differently. It gave me chills, like a cold bucket of water pouring over my head. I listened to it over and over again, torturing myself. 'It's Not My Time' was predicting the future. I didn't deserve to be there and I would never win.

Despite all this, I wasn't trained to quit. After the wedding, after the depression, I got back in the water and into my best ever form. I was an elite athlete, and I could push the darkness away. *I'm strong, I'm fit, I'm healthy, therefore I'm fast.* While all this negativity was churning, another part of my brain was thinking about Kieren Perkins at the Atlanta Olympics in 1996, coming in from the outside lane to claim his gold medal in the 1500-metre freestyle. He had very nearly missed the final too because he'd messed up in the heats. He had had a panic attack too. Been consumed by self-doubt. If Kieren could come back from the outside lane, I could do it. I just had to focus. All of this would end up being a funny story, just some dramatic tension on my 'road to glory'. *No doubts, no regrets, I'm just here to have fun.*

It's not that the dark side was winning, but it was warring hard. And to be at the top of my game as an elite athlete, the noise in my head had to stop. I needed to be that finely tuned machine, inside and out, calmly stepping through the process, stripped back to the bare essentials. That's what was going on when I raced, behind the golden girl smile. I was running a simple, clean, effective mental program, sparse but razor-sharp. What happened after the semi-finals was that my parasympathetic nervous system kicked in and my body and brain got stuck in a 'fight or flight' response. I was doing nothing in my dorm room as I waited overnight for the finals, but my body was under massive stress as I struggled to control my panic and negativity. It was exhausting. It broke me in a way that swimming never had. I had been trained to deal with emotional fatigue throughout my career, but the sharp emotional roller-coaster I had been on after the semi-final was just too much. I fell into fog— it felt like a heavy, damp blanket was covering my body, a physical and emotional fatigue that wouldn't lift.

I slept as best as I could, but I was tired the next morning when I was preparing for the race. I was no longer the favourite. Yes, I was still the world record holder, but there were others in the centre lanes—Natalie Coughlin, Britta Steffen and Marleen Veldhuis. I didn't have to worry about them; the main thing I was up against was my own inner turmoil. Ironically, I didn't really understand how much it was affecting me. I prided myself on my ability to let things go and get into the zone, so I felt confident that I would be able to perform when it counted. But my desperation to win the 100-metre freestyle was overwhelming, and not in a positive way. I just couldn't let it go.

There is a crucial moment when you have done all your training, all your preparation, and you just have to let your body take over. When the gun went off, I was still desperately trying to control everything, and that was how I raced.

I went out far too hard from the block, smashing ferociously through the first 35 metres. My legs felt tight at the 35-metre mark, which was a problem. When I pushed off the wall at 50 metres, I knew I was done. I was totally shattered. And what was worse was that the thought was crystal-clear in my head: *I'm absolutely screwed*. In my best races, I remembered nothing but the feeling of being in the water. My mind was gone completely, my body on autopilot. But I remember every thought I had during the 100-metre final, and each one was filled with doubt. I was losing the race in my head.

When I came off the wall, my legs were like jelly. *This is hard. I have to knuckle down*. At the 75-metre mark, my arms were dead weights in the water. *Just keep going*, I thought. *Just keep going*. At 95 metres I felt like I had come to a complete stop, just dead in the water. The voice in my head was screaming, *Get there, get there, get there!* I was fighting myself until the very end.

As it turned out, I led for the entire race, but Britta Steffen caught me in the final stroke. She touched the wall milliseconds ahead of me—0.04 of a second to be exact. It wasn't my time, after all.

It wasn't just a bad day. I wasn't worthy. In my head, I was so shit at the sport that I couldn't even put together a decent race in the final. I didn't belong there, I didn't deserve to be there, I didn't have what it takes to win. The gold medal I had won in the butterfly two days earlier meant nothing. No one had expected me to win the fly, so I felt it didn't really count. Freestyle was my race and I had thrown it away. I couldn't help but feel embarrassed.

The hardest thing and the best thing about being a swimmer is that it's all on you. If you win, it's your victory— but if you fuck up, that's also on you. You've got no one else to blame, no one else to point the finger at. If you swim a perfect race and come second, you can't complain; you can be disappointed, but you know that you did your best. But to know that I had stuffed up the entire race process, and then to come second by such a tiny fraction of time . . . it felt like such a terrible waste. I had prided myself on being such a tough competitor but it turned out I was one of those people who crumbled under pressure. *What was the point of any of this? Why am I even here?*

I did my best to hide the disappointment. For all of my grief, I understood that there were thousands of people who would kill to win a silver medal at the Olympics, and I certainly didn't want to take away from Britta's achievement or spoil her moment. But I was choking back tears on the podium as the German national anthem played. My eyes were red from all the crying I had done in the bathroom before the ceremony—I saw it later in the photos. I didn't want to be a sore loser, on top of everything else, but I was shattered. And at the same time, I was ashamed that I felt bad in a moment that should have been filled with pride. Silver is still silver, in the hardest race in the world. That day, it was just another stick on the bonfire of my self-esteem, which was quietly burning to the ground.

In the final days of competition in Beijing, I had the heats and semis for the 50-metre freestyle and the 4x100 metre medley. The 50-metre freestyle was always my celebration race. I always did well. I had always medalled. And that's what I was telling myself, desperately clinging to whatever I could to get me through to the end of the Games.

I made it through the heats and semis of the 50-metre freestyle, but I knew I had lost my edge. The fatigue was like chains, weighing me down. I didn't have that reserve of energy to increase my speed as I progressed from the heats to the semis to the final, which is what normally happened. Normally, I would go into the final with extra gas in my tank, twitchy and fast. But my limbs were heavy. I was off my game. I just kept telling myself, *This is my race. This is my medal—I can do it.*

Logically, I know I swam a good race in the final. I did the best race I could with what I had in the tank, but I just wasn't fast enough. I came fourth in the end, and it wasn't even a shock. My mind had pulled my body so low that fourth was the best I could manage. And when I climbed out of the pool, I was so sad and so dark that I thought I would never be okay.

Fifteen minutes later, with my teammates rallying around me, I swam freestyle in the 4x100-metre medley. I wanted to be there for my teammates, so I asked them for help and they embraced me, physically and emotionally. They reached down and pulled me up out of the dark. I couldn't have had better women around me in that moment, young as they were. Emily Seebohm, Leisel Jones and Jess Schipper pulled me into the race process, buoyed my confidence with jokes and laughter, and reminded me that I was one of them—one of the best athletes in the world. And together, we went on to win a gold medal. Not my medal, but ours.

I wish I had been able to enjoy the success I had in Beijing in the moment. I wish I hadn't been so blinkered, so desperate, so cruel to myself. In the end, I won two golds, a bronze and a silver, which I can now say with utter sincerity was an incredible achievement. I know that now—I've figured it out. It was just so devastating at the time.

Chapter Seven

2015

'This, too, shall pass.'

—Unknown

I don't have a tidal wave of love for Poppy—that's not my experience. It grows a little more every day. It's a relationship that builds over time, as I get to know her—the little sounds she makes, the colour of her eyes. I feel connected to her, so I'm not worried about the slow way my heart opens up. I'm just learning about my kid. Curious. I feel deep in my bones that she is mine. It's the same for Luke—I can see it on his face when he holds her—and it makes me so happy knowing that we are a family.

The first few nights in the hospital are a bit messy—Poppy is cluster-feeding every twenty minutes, all night long—but I'm delighted that she latched immediately to breastfeed.

A girlfriend of mine had to transfer to formula pretty quickly because, as can so easily happen, breastfeeding just didn't work out. It's a relief that everything is going smoothly for me. The breastfeeding creates a ton of serotonin, so I have happy hormones coursing through my body, and I have nurses taking care of me around the clock, and food being delivered. I didn't tear during the birth, and a lot of my water weight dropped during the sweat and fluid rush of the birthing process, so I'm recovering fast.

We have so many visitors, it's overwhelming. You lose a fair amount of dignity when you're pushing a bowling ball out of your vagina in front of six people, but I'm not used to pulling a boob out in front of people. Even though it's mostly family and friends, I feel a twinge of self-consciousness every time. But it's amazing to introduce Poppy to people, and to see the joy on their faces. Seeing my daughter in my mother's arms for the first time is a powerful and heart-warming thing.

I'm nervous about leaving the hospital. *Are they actually going to let us take a human baby home?* I wonder. *Don't they know we don't know anything?* We don't have a neck brace in the baby capsule—we figured it was overkill—but I can see Poppy's head lolling to the side every time we go around a corner and I think, *Oh shit, we're going to kill her.* Luke drives 40 kilometres an hour all the way home.

I've read *What to Expect When You're Expecting*, but it was mostly about pregnancy, coming to an abrupt halt right when things start to get interesting. I know other mums so I have a network. My sister Justine's kids—Matty, Ruby and James—are three, five and seven. My sister-in-law Georgie has eight-month-old Emma and two-year-old Lucy. My friend Jess has a three-month-old, Mia, and my friend Alice, with whom I used to compete in Olympic relays and win on the world stage, has four-week-old Vance. I turn to all of them with questions, and they give me useful and sympathetic answers—more sympathy than I'd ever had for them before I had walked in their shoes. I had no idea what they were going through. I realise that all the mums I have known have been glossing over the details, and I didn't know enough to dig for more information, or offer them more support. Now that I'm a mother, my respect for them is leagues deep. I only wish I'd asked more questions before I stepped through the front door of my house with a newborn in my arms.

I'm learning everything from scratch, which is terrifying. And just when I think I have a handle on something, Poppy's routine changes, or she changes, and I feel like I'm back at square one. Babies are such mysterious little things. There's so much thinking that has to happen, which is quite overwhelming. I have to pay such close attention all the time, just to understand what's going on. *Are you wet? Are you hungry? Have you done a poo? Are you too cold? Are you too hot? Why are you grizzling?* I really haven't been much of a thinker, so it's like the muscle is underdeveloped, and this constant vigilance, constant learning, is exhausting.

Luke goes back to work a week after we come home. We made the decision together and I am perfectly happy with it— Luke runs the business alone, so if he's not working, nobody is. He takes responsibility for all the laundry, which is a considerable job because we thought we'd try using cloth nappies. The rest of the house quickly becomes a bombsite. Poppy is doing well at night, solid two-hour blocks between feeds, but she doesn't sleep much during the day, so it's hard to get anything done. She will sleep for 40 minutes at a time during the day, at the most, and she never really settles properly, so I'm lucky if I can manage a shower or a quick bowl of cereal before three o'clock in the afternoon. She's doesn't have colic, nothing that severe, but I would describe my daughter as a cranky baby. The other newborns I know seem super chilled by comparison—good sleepers, and seemingly always content. I try not to make comparisons, though, as I know it doesn't help.

Two weeks in, I get the baby blues, just the natural dip that comes as the tide of birth hormones start to leech out of your body. Luke walks in the door after work and I hand him the baby and burst into tears. 'Oh my god, what's wrong?' he asks.

'Nothing, we had a good day,' I sob. 'I have no idea why I'm crying.'

It's not rational, it's just my body taking over. But I decide that we need to get a dummy. A lot of the literature says that dummies are a bad idea before the baby is six weeks old and breastfeeding is established, because they can create something called 'nipple confusion'. But while we were doing very well with the breastfeeding, the days are full of fretful, cranky, unsettled whimpering, and I don't think it's good for me or Pops. A dummy helps considerably.

She needs to be moved every few minutes and entertained constantly—which, by the way, I find can be terribly boring. All mothers, I discover, learn this pretty quickly. Your baby, the pride and joy of your life, is actually kind of dull from moment to moment. Of course, it feels like an incredible privilege to watch her develop and grow, and every time she does something new, my heart jumps a little. But again, I had visions of binge-watching televisions shows I had missed while I was at home on maternity leave, relaxing and cuddling my baby, and drinking cups of tea, but every ten minutes Poppy and I have something else to do—a change, a feed, a walk, a burp, a little bounce, a change of scenery. This routine kicks off at 5 a.m. and continues pretty much unbroken until early evening, day after day, which requires quite a bit of endurance. I've always been better at sprints.

At least we're mobile. From when Poppy was about nine days old, I started taking her out. We visit my mum or catch up with friends for coffee, and go for long walks in the park. It adds to my general tiredness, but it doesn't feel unmanageable to me. Come six weeks, Poppy is sleeping eight to ten hours a night, which is just marvellous. She still doesn't sleep during the day, but what a masterful night sleeper she is, and it's amazing how well I can cope when I've had a decent night's sleep. All in all, I'd say it's a challenge but I'm up to it. *I think I'm nailing this motherhood thing.*

If Poppy holds my finger, I think, *Oh my god, you are literally the most beautiful thing in the world and I cannot deal with how much I love you.* Two minutes later, I think, *Oh Christ, why are you being such a little shit—why won't you stop crying?* The extremes are wild, but both reactions are completely honest, and it genuinely can happen that fast. She goes from gooing and gahing to doing explosive poos in a heartbeat, and my feelings do the same. It's intense. All the feelings are happening at once.

I know this experience is universal. I am not special. I'm no longer the golden girl athlete I once was, with the eyes of the world on me. I'm a mum like all mums, which is fine. It's great. Except, actually, as time goes on, I wonder if it's completely true. Poppy doesn't stop grizzling. It actually gets worse, which is really difficult. She needs constant attention and distraction, whereas my friends seem to have these placid, docile babies, and she rarely seems completely happy for more than a passing moment. I'm used to getting feedback for my work, and the feedback she's giving me isn't great. But I don't know how to course-correct or improve my performance. I'm starting to feel like she's annoyed with me, or annoyed at something that I can't fix. And a deep, subconscious thought starts to take root: *I'm not good at this.*

I'm especially thrilled when she progresses a little, because I'm doing all this work. When she smiles for the first time, when she lifts her head just a little bit, it feels like everything is worthwhile. I weigh Poppy every week just to get some sense that things are moving forward. It's something tangible I can see, a number on the scale, and it gives me an enormous sense of pride and satisfaction. I realise that there is still an athlete in me trying to control an outcome, echoes of who I was in a past life that need to fall away. Meanwhile, I'm attending a baby sensory class every Monday to learn how to play with Poppy better. On Tuesdays, I attend a mother's group to try to connect with other people like me. What I learn is that every baby progresses at different stages, and every baby has its own challenges. Me and my baby, we've got to be our own team. Assuming she doesn't hate me.

I feel quite smug about the fact that Poppy has slept through the night from such an early age. I assume I must have established some great routine with her—that it was somehow my doing—so it's a little disconcerting when, at four months old, she starts waking every two hours at night. I have no idea why it's happening and I have no idea how to stop it.

They talk about a four-month sleep progression, so maybe that's what we're dealing with. Whatever it is, it gets worse and worse over the next few weeks. We go from a full night of unbroken sleep to 1.5-hour blocks, slowly, incrementally, unfolding over days. An hour and a half, and then she wakes up and cries, and only the boob will calm her. An hour and a half is the most sleep I will get before I wake up to settle her again.

By the time Poppy is five months old, I have begun to dread the night. I'm just so tired, so incredibly tired, but I know I won't be able to sleep. I can't face the idea of getting up to feed all through the night; I'm starting to feel delirious, and I've been falling asleep on the couch while breastfeeding, which, as every mother is warned, can be incredibly dangerous. Several nights in a row I start to cry after dinner. Luke is alarmed, but he doesn't understand. How can it possibly be worse when the sun goes down? I'm with Poppy all day too. 'I just don't want night to come,' I weep. At night it's dark, it's quiet, I'm all alone. The only thing I can think to do is to google 'Why won't my baby sleep?'

I start co-sleeping with Poppy to try to cope, in the second bedroom so that we don't disturb Luke, but very quickly after I move she regresses from windows of an hour and a half to blocks of just 45 minutes. Something has gone very wrong with my baby and I have no idea how to fix it. Even though I am next to her in the bed and I don't have to get up, my sleep is always broken, fitful, always filtered with the sound of Poppy crying and the anxiety that I will never catch up. I feed her every 45 minutes, but I know she's not hungry; she just can't settle herself without being attached. She falls asleep on my breast, then the nipple falls out of her mouth, and as her natural 45-minute sleep cycle passes, she realises that something has changed, comes out of her sleep and starts wailing. It's not a gentle whimper—she cries with rage until I wake up and settle her.

Some nights I fall straight back to sleep as soon as she's attached, but sometimes I am just so fucking angry and frustrated and exhausted that I am flooded with adrenaline and I just can't get to sleep again. My nerves are like rubber bands, stretched to breaking point. And while I'm not sleeping properly, neither is poor Poppy. Every day she is more tired, more aggravated, more distressed and therefore more difficult to soothe. We're locked together in a slow downward spiral.

During the day, I'm a zombie, and decision fatigue begins to set in. All the micro questions I have to answer are completely overwhelming. *Is she tired? Is she wet? Does she have wind? Does she need to feed? Has she had enough?* I can barely think my way through Poppy's needs, let alone my own. *Have I had a shower? Do I need to eat? Have I brushed my teeth? Have I had any water today? What should I make for dinner? What do we need from the supermarket?* I know I have to make these decisions but

I physically can't get there. My mind is blank, blocked—I can't focus. Every minor decision feels like climbing a mountain.

I start to go days without showering. Physically, I don't have the energy. Mentally, I don't have the energy. Poppy's awake all the time, so it would have to happen when she's awake, and she will wail and scream the whole time, which feels like more trouble than it's worth.

Luke doesn't understand the co-sleeping. He can see that I'm doing badly but he thinks I'm making things harder than they need to be. 'What are you doing?' he keeps asking me. 'You're not coping, Lib.' He is frustrated that I won't consider a different approach, but for some reason I believe in attachment parenting, or at least I think I do. I just can't let my baby cry—everybody tells you that it releases chemicals in their brain that can cause permanent harm. Controlled crying is out, sleep training is out, anything that means Poppy would be left alone to scream. In my heart and soul, I just don't feel it's right. But by the time she is six months old, I am coming apart at the edges.

If I could somehow do better, I know she would be fine. She would settle, and she would sleep. If I could be better, she'd be fine, but I'm failing her. I know I'm failing her. I can't say it out loud, or even consciously acknowledge it to myself, but I am failing as a mother. I am so ashamed.

As a swimmer, I had control. I got the feedback, I saw the analysis, I knew where I could improve and I did it, and

I saw results. Now I spend many late nights on the internet, looking for answers. I keep hoping something will change, but this situation is completely out of my control. And I can't bring myself to ask for help. Mum knows that I'm struggling, my sisters know, but they don't know how bad it is, really. We aren't seeing a paediatrician. I'm not seeing a doctor. I keep persevering, alone, always optimistic that tonight things will change and Poppy will sleep. My optimism is brutal, in its own way, because it is always foolish, and every single night it fails over and over, and that only makes me feel worse.

Luke and I are fighting, and he's approaching his own breaking point, so we agree that we'll try something different at some point. I tell him ten months—if we get to ten months and nothing has changed, maybe we can try something else. I don't want to think about it yet, and anyway I'm struggling to think clearly about anything. I wish he could understand how important it is to me to do the best thing for my baby.

For five months, I don't sleep. We don't get a breast pump and collect milk so that Luke can feed her during the night and I can sleep, because he is a new father who doesn't know to suggest it and I am a bit of a martyr about it all. He's the one who has to get up and go to work. He has a front-row seat to this unfolding shit-show, and he doesn't know how to help. 'She'll cry if we do sleep training, Lib, but she's crying anyway—what difference does it make?' My stubbornness about co-sleeping feels like the only thing I have left to hold on to. It's the only thing left that I can control.

There are no pure moments anymore. Sometimes Poppy will smile at me or laugh and I will feel a little leap in my heart, but it is always tinged with exhaustion and sadness. She looks so tired, too. There are dark rings around her eyes. I regret doing this to her. I regret having her, too.

I am so often angry with Poppy. I know that there are times when I am too rough when I pick her up. My thoughts have become really dark as well. These grim ideas that just appear out of nowhere. Sometimes, when she cries, I imagine hurting her. I have this clear mental picture of throwing her out of an open window. And I am alone with the avalanche of shame and the horror that follows. No one can ever know.

The only life raft I have to cling to is something Rob said to me when we brought Poppy in for her six-week check-up, after she was born: 'Have you felt like leaving her on the side of the road yet?' I knew he was being light-hearted and I laughed weakly, but the conversation keeps replaying in my head, and it gives me some comfort. I am not crazy. I know it is normal to feel stressed, conflicted, even regretful that I ever had a child.

I know, too, that I will never hurt my daughter. There are times when I have to put her in her cot and just walk away, but at least I have the presence of mind to do that. I have an amazing support network and I am mentally healthy enough to have some control over these thoughts, but it is suddenly clear to me how it could happen. I am still relatively reasonable and rational and logical, and yet I have these urges. I understand now how some women can kill their babies. It's obviously something that is incredibly tragic and devastating for any family, and something that our brains naturally recoil from contemplating, but if I was severely depressed, if I had no emotional support, would I be able to control myself? I don't know. I am suddenly filled with deep compassion for these women, who had seemed like monsters to me before.

There isn't a day when I don't get out of bed. I do what I have to do, but I am bitter and angry, and resistant to what this situation is, and so, so angry with Poppy. My thoughts are morphing from guilt to frustration that I've been saddled with such a difficult child. *What's wrong with you? Why can't you just be easier?* I'm struggling to spend time with friends with small babies because it makes me feel even worse to see how effortless their children seem compared to Poppy. I wear a bright smile at our coffee dates and laugh away their friendly enquiries about how we're both getting along—'Oh, you know, not too bad, could do with a decent night's sleep, haha'—but inside I feel resentful and ashamed, always on the verge of tears. It's a weakness that I can't admit to even my closest friends, and I know it's not something people can really understand unless they've been through it.

What are we going to do about Poppy? She's eight months old and this conversation is happening almost daily between me and Luke, the two of us struggling to connect as we fight over the same ground again and again. I have started to hint at the dark thoughts I've had in my conversations with him, but he has no patience for me anymore—he knows that sleep will help, and he wants us to do sleep training. *Here is the problem, here is the solution—what is the issue with that?* I know he doesn't understand the emotional side of things, the guilt I am feeling, but I am beginning to weaken. I just don't have a choice. If I don't consider some other options, I don't know what will happen.

My sister-in-law recommends a sleep consultant for babies, Katie Forsythe of the Baby Sleep Company in Brisbane. I start following her on social media, trawling through her website on those long, sleepless nights, just beginning to consider whether this is a path I could ever go down. I'm still holding out hope that Poppy will just change, because the literature on attachment parenting says that all babies start sleeping through eventually. It says we shouldn't consider it a problem when babies don't sleep through the night, and we certainly shouldn't 'train' them with brutal traumatic crying episodes that flood them with cortisol until they 'give up' and go to sleep.

The Facebook groups and forums that are in favour of attachment parenting are always on my mind, with their seemingly strict views on neonatal health. Naturally, I don't want to cause psychological damage to my baby. But I'm noticing more and more that those attachment parenting groups rarely talk about the mother's health, which increasingly seems bizarre to me. How on earth can my baby be safe and stable if I am falling to pieces? Are mothers supposed to sacrifice themselves completely? Is that meant to be noble? I have a deep sense of responsibility to my child, but my sense of needing to measure up to these ill-fitting ideals is starting to fall away.

In her video posts and her advice online, Katie seems genuinely concerned for the health of both mother and baby. There is no one-size-fits-all philosophy—she emphasises that every situation is different, and different approaches could be beneficial. Part of me is ashamed to even be considering this stuff, but Katie's philosophy is incredibly forgiving, and that feels like kindness to me right now. Everything she posts is non-judgemental. I couldn't bear talking to someone about what we've been through, only to have them tell me everything I've done wrong; the negative voices in my head are loud enough. At some point, I decide that if we are going to do sleep training, Katie is the only person I could trust.

In the meantime, I am trying to focus a little bit more on self-care. I'm enrolled in a mums and bubs class at the gym because I know that, for me, not exercising is making everything that much worse. I need so badly to be moving my body and getting some endorphins pumping through my system, but it has been so hard to fit any exercise in, and so hard to push my exhausted body. I need it, though. It's really important to me. It's really important to my peace of mind.

One morning when Poppy is eight and a half months old, I put her in her car seat and get ready to drive to the gym across town for our class. Poppy has always hated being in the car and we've spun her car seat around to face forward, earlier than recommended, to try to keep her calm. I'm worried about my driving ability because I'm so sleep-deprived and at an emotional breaking point, but the only way I can manage Pops while we're in the car is if she is facing forward. I'm constantly reaching back to give her a dummy or give her something to play with, while feeling like I have tunnel vision and I can't focus on anything clearly.

I'm worried about having a car accident. I'm worried Poppy won't be safe, but I'm also keenly aware that I need to be able to see her face. If I can't see her face, she becomes less human to me, just a disembodied scream. It's the same at night: I have to keep a light on at all times so I can see her, because I feel like I'm going to hurt her if I can't see her face. The sound makes me crazy. I need to see her face to remember that she is my daughter and to block out the dark, impulsive thoughts that sometimes rush into my head whispering, *This is how—this is how you make it stop.*

I know I'll feel better if I go to the gym—I always do—but really I am on autopilot. I just need to get out of the house and Poppy will have to come, whether she likes the car or not. She's crying before the car door is shut beside her, and crying as we back out of the driveway. It builds to a piercing wail as we set off down the street. I start signing 'The Grand Old Duke of York', because it sometimes helps, but my voice is thin and wavering. We had a particularly bad night the night before. I sing it over and over again, but it isn't helping. Poppy's shrill wailing continues unbroken as we drive through the streets of Seven Hills.

The drive is long, nearly half an hour, and five minutes in, it's like I have some kind of break. Something deep inside me snaps. I keep driving towards the gym, but some hysterical emotion grips me, and I begin screaming at my daughter. *Shut up! Fucking shut up! You're not taking this away from me—I'm going to the fucking gym, you little shit!* I don't know if I have actually spoken the words aloud or if I'm just making a wordless, shrieking noise. But I am screaming and screaming at her, at the top of my lungs, for the remainder of the drive. Twenty minutes, more, of white-hot rage, creating a feedback loop with Poppy's screaming, which only gets louder. I am screaming my hatred for Poppy, blind with anger. My daughter hates me, she is punishing me, and I hate her for it. I hate her.

I am unsafe on the road, completely out of control, but I keep driving. A minute before we arrive at the gym, Poppy falls asleep. She literally passes out from exhaustion, from the effort of screaming her lungs out. I pull into a parking bay and immediately begin weeping—deep, harsh, broken sobs. The sound coming out of me is keening, brutal. I am a terrible mother. I am a failure. The world would be better without me in it. Poppy deserves better than me.

I am at rock bottom. I know now that I need to get help, though I don't even know what that means. I have absolutely nothing left in me. I can't keep going like this.

2009

'She stood in the storm and when the wind did
not blow her away, she adjusted her sails.'

—Elizabeth Edwards

I took an extended break after Beijing. It wasn't clear to me whether or not I should keep swimming. And if I did, would I keep training with Stephan? My dream had always been that I would reach the pinnacle of my sport and retire a champion. I had assumed Beijing would be my last Olympics, but I had also assumed that I would leave that competition completely satisfied. Instead, I was almost grieving. For the second time, I had failed to win the gold medal in the 100-metre freestyle in the only arena that truly counted. I felt like I had unfinished business at a time when I had imagined I would be done.

Part of the problem was that I didn't know what was next. I knew that I had to retire at some point, but there was nothing beyond that; it was like the future was shrouded in some kind of cloud and I couldn't really think my way through it. I wasn't nervous about what would come after swimming because I wasn't thinking about it at all. My thoughts were instead consumed by whether or not I needed something more from the sport.

As I was taking time off to think through all of this— three months in total—there was some movement at the club. I read in the newspaper that Stephan had taken on a new recruit after Beijing. Jess Schipper was moving from the Redcliffe Leagues Lawnton Club, where she had trained under Ken Wood, to join Stephan's team at the Commercial Swimming Club in Fortitude Valley. She was a major rival of mine, my closest Australian competitor in the butterfly, and it was shocking to me that Stephan would consider training her without talking to me about it first. I didn't expect him to make a decision based on my feelings, but surely I had warranted a phone call. I couldn't believe I had to find out about it in the paper.

It felt like Stephan had chosen Jess over me. I was always an emotional person, and he was the closest thing I had to a father figure, with my own father so detached and absent, so I experienced the news as a deep kind of rejection. I was 23 years old and I had been swimming with Stephan since I was seventeen. We'd had a long career together, in swimming terms, and I'd just assumed it would continue. I wondered, like I had with my father, what I had done wrong.

The year prior to Beijing I had started asking Stephan a lot more questions in training. I wanted to be a bit more autonomous and own the process more, which made me less compliant and more combative. He was frustrated by this and we clashed repeatedly, but I still thought we were on the same team. Human relationships are complicated, and they become more complicated the deeper they get, and Stephan and I saw each other between three and seven hours a day, six days a week, 48 weeks a year. We knew how to push each other's buttons, sure, but I thought we were closer than we had ever been. Maybe I misunderstood our relationship. Maybe he had just lost faith in me. Maybe I would have been okay with it, if he'd just picked up the phone.

I'm sure from his perspective—he was so clinical, so pragmatic—it wasn't a big deal. And it was obviously a sound business decision to take Jess on, since he didn't know if I was coming back. He had to think about his own career as a coach, and Jess was an incredibly gifted swimmer—he would have been mad to turn her away when she came to him for training. Part of my brain understood this, of course, but it was drowned out by the hurt. I had to have a conversation with Stephan.

I went down to the pool and sat opposite him and told him how I felt, and of course he was surprised to learn that his decision had cut me so badly. But he was very matter-of-fact in his reply. Jess was committed to the next four years of training, to get to the London Olympics. Stephan still didn't know where I stood, and he needed to move forward. It felt like a slap in the face, but I couldn't fault his logic. I still didn't know what I wanted to do. I only knew that it was the end of the line for Stephan and me, after five years together.

I had so much to be grateful for. You need to have a good connection with your coach: if you're happy, you want to celebrate, and if you're not happy, you want a soft place to fall. The only fault I could ever find with Stephan was that he was never that soft place. It was always, 'Why did you do that? This is how we do better.' He was always on, always goal-oriented. Sometimes it felt cold. Sometimes I just needed him to understand that I was a human being and not a machine, and that it was important for me to take a moment to process what was happening to me. But on the other hand, looking back, I know it would only have made things worse if he had indulged me. If he had opened that door even a fraction and allowed me to wallow in my grief, to throw myself a little pity party every time something didn't go my way, I would have just stayed there. Because I have such big emotions, there was always the risk of getting lost in them. Stephan's clinical attitude always pushed me out of the dark.

It wasn't more than a couple of weeks later that I decided to go back to swimming. I'm not sure what my real motivation was; things were still so muddled in my head. I wanted to take care of unfinished business, I suppose, and I wanted to prove to Stephan that I could do it without him. Also, I didn't have any better ideas for what I should be doing with my time. I was never any good at really digging through my emotional and psychological experiences. I was an athlete, trained to focus and move forward, so I took that impulse and ran with it.

The problem was that there were no real alternatives in terms of coaching in Queensland. Simon Cusack was probably the only option, but he was training Cate and Bronte Campbell over at Indooroopilly Swimming Club, and they were Olympic-class sprinters, just like me. Cate had won bronze in the 50-metre freestyle in Beijing, and Bronte was coming up fast behind her. Much like with Jess, I wouldn't have felt comfortable training with girls who were my direct competitors.

Luke and I decided that moving to Sydney was our only real option if I was going to continue swimming. We had always assumed that we would live there after I retired, out of some vague sense that I would get work in the television industry, which was largely Sydney-based. Plus, Luke's family was there and his business prospects were good, so he wouldn't be disadvantaged. And I'd recently learned that a coach named Grant Stoelwinder was moving to the New South Wales Institute of Sport. He was going to build a top-flight professional squad around a swimmer named Eamon Sullivan, who had won two silvers and a bronze medal in Beijing, in similar races to mine. It sounded like the perfect environment for me, as a step towards retirement. A new coach would be invigorating but I would be swimming with tried and tested athletes who had some maturity and experience in addition to raw talent. What I needed, I assumed, was a change of scenery.

We moved to Sydney in December 2008, and I became the only female swimmer on Grant's team. Our job was swimming and the training was structured to reflect that —swimming didn't come second to study or some other kind of work. We kept professional hours, or thereabouts, arriving for training at 7 a.m. rather than 5.30 a.m. We'd be in the pool from seven until nine, then hit the gym for an hour or so before going home for lunch and then returning in the afternoon for another block of training sessions. I struggled with the routine because there wasn't enough of a gap for me to rest and recover between sessions, but the guys seemed to thrive. Besides Eamon, there was Andrew Lauterstein, Garth Kates, Matt and Andrew Abood, and Geoff Huegill—all powerhouse swimmers who were extremely focused on beating their way to the top.

Despite the promise of professionalism and the very serious boys I was training with, my athletic career felt less taxing in Sydney than it had in Brisbane. Grant (we called him Stolly) and Stephan had what felt like radically differ-ent styles, and I found training under Stolly to be much easier, in a sense. His approach was based on quality rather than endurance—high-intensity sessions, but fewer of them. I also felt like I was under less scrutiny for my technique and form, probably because Stephan for so many years had been so incredibly intense. Stolly wanted us to race fresh and at higher levels throughout the season, rather than smashing our bodies, tapering and springing from a tight coil in competition. It was a perfectly valid system and he was known for training champions, but it was just so much less demanding than what I was used to. Ironically, I lost quite a lot of fitness, but I raced very fast under his guidance.

It was challenging being the only girl on the squad, and not just because the guys' physical capacity so far outstripped my own. The real problem was that they were all really quite cool, and I was a bit of a nerd. I had a very daggy energy, and they were like a pack of strapping young gods. They were all confident, single and sleek as seals, and it affected the way they carried themselves and the way they interacted with me. We didn't share a sense of humour. One-on-one, we could joke around and be friendly, because they were actually very sweet people, but I found them a little alienat-ing as a pack. We also didn't share the same interests. Lauto was a DJ in his spare time, Eamon was deeply into food, and Skippy (Geoff Huegill) was just a very social animal and was constantly tackling the next business opportunity. I never felt like I was part of a family. We were friendly but not friends, which made things harder than I'd imagined they would be, because I really didn't know anyone else in Sydney.

Surprisingly, although he had lived in Sydney for most of his life, Luke was also quite socially isolated. During the four years he'd been in Brisbane, Luke had lost touch with his schoolfriends, and he was now focused more on his new business plan rather than on making friends. In the fallout from the Global Financial Crisis, Luke wanted to start a new investment fund based on the principle of alignment, where he made money only when his investors did. But, as you can imagine, there's a planet of red tape you have to navigate before you can start trading with other people's money, so much of his time was consumed with setting up the business.

It wasn't much of a life. Luke worked, I swam and in the evenings we flaked out in front of the television. We couldn't afford to do anything else. We lived in a small cottage in the inner west, in Lilyfield, close to the Ian Thorpe Aquatic Centre and Homebush, where I was training. It was $750 for what was technically a three-bedroom house, but we referred to the third bedroom as the 'couch room' because our couch was the only thing that fitted in there. We could reach out the side window and touch the neighbour's house. Everything in Sydney was either hard to get to or really expensive, so we didn't have much quality of life after the rent had been paid.

We felt very optimistic going into the move, but life in Sydney soon became very lonely, very quickly. I had a lot of time on my hands to sit and think about what I was doing with my life and with my swimming, and I found I was always ill-at-ease for some reason. I couldn't find my groove. I enrolled in an online course in marketing and communication, but it was just something I thought I should do. I was completely unmotivated about study—I was just trying to fill some hours in the day.

A big part of the problem was that we just weren't well suited to Sydney. It felt frantic compared to Brisbane: high-energy, high-paced and highly competitive. And it all felt so superficial to Luke and me. It didn't help that we were so far from family and friends, cooped up together in our tiny house.

There were other issues as well. Luke was so focused on building his business that everything else seemed to fade from his attention a bit, including me. For so long we had been such great friends and partners, and had shared so many of the highs and lows of our young lives together. Now I felt like he was travelling in a different direction, and wasn't including me on his journey. He felt cold and distant, like my father, like Stephan. I didn't know where the warmth between us had gone.

The other big issue contributing to the cracks in our relationship was money, which again felt directly related to Luke's work. It wasn't just that the rent was exorbitant, but our income was slowing and Luke had invested all our savings in the stock market—that's why we were renting. In the meantime, Luke's business was still in its formative stage, which meant he was earning nothing from it. We lived on the money from my swimming endorsements, but the boomtime surrounding the Olympic Games had come to an end, so the river of income was dwindling to a stream. It added pressure that we didn't need when we both felt quite unhappy, which was only heightened by the long stretches we spent apart in 2009, as I travelled often for swimming meets. Stolly wanted us racing us much as possible, including professional tours like the Mare Nostrum and the Paris International. There was a three-week training camp in Italy at one point. Cumulatively, I spent at least three months away that year.

My swimming career was going well, or it appeared to be. I looked like I was in condition and I was racing well, but in the back of my mind I didn't necessarily feel that I could progress much further under Stolly's tutelage. I was still an elite athlete, one of the fastest women in the sport, but the ferocity and hunger that had fuelled my early career had started to wane, though it was difficult to see that at the time. To me, it felt like the whole sport was changing, not just my place in it. And this was driven home in July 2009, at the World Championships in Rome.

*

I was an ambassador for Speedo, but much like the rest of the Australian swimming team, I was under pressure to wear a full-body swimsuit made by another company that became known in the press as the 'super suit'. It was made of thick rubber and felt like a wetsuit, covering my body from shoulder to ankle. The minute I put it on and jumped in the pool, I knew it would give swimmers an unfair advantage. The thickness of the material gave you additional buoyancy, and that meant you'd expend less energy staying afloat, which could make you more efficient in the water. It was clear to me that people would race much faster wearing the super suits, which of course was clearly the intention. Tests were done that demonstrated that the suits were performance-enhancing, but for some reason they were ignored by FINA and by Swimming Australia, as well as many other peak swimming organisations around the globe. Every team adopted them, because no one wanted to be at a disadvantage in international competition. I guess they figured it wasn't cheating if everyone was doing it.

Jaked, the company that manufactured the performance-enhancing suits, was based in Italy, and with the World Championships taking place in Rome, I assumed that everyone would be keen to have a spectacular year in the pool. And the company got exactly what it was hoping for with one record-breaking swim after another. In fact, every single world record was broken that year, except for the men's 1500-metre freestyle.

Against Stolly's advice, I made a decision not to wear the super suit in my individual races. It was a team decision for the relay and I went along with the team, but I just didn't feel right about it at any point—in fact, the whole thing made me incredibly depressed. I didn't make any grand announcement in the media, I just suited up in my usual swimsuit, feeling at least like my own integrity was intact. As the week of the World Championships went on, there was increasing speculation in the media about the effect the suits were having on these suddenly accelerated performances, not just from the top-ranked swimmers but from the top sixteen. The tone of the discussion was a little sour, or it seemed that way to me, as though the whole sport was tarnished.

I had worked my entire career on my starts, turns and finishes. I'd put in gruelling hours of training to hone those skills, which gave me a competitive edge. My free swim and my back-end speeds were strong, but it was the starts, turns and finishes that made me the athlete that I was, and it was a long, hard road to the top of the pile. The super suits allowed people who weren't necessarily good at starts, turns and finishes to become good at those skills overnight. It allowed people who had taken three-month breaks after Beijing to still do significant personal best times—to become instantly far better swimmers than they had been a day before. The public seemed underwhelmed by any race that wasn't a record-breaker, which devalued the amazing achievements of all the incredible swimmers who came before. *Do you know how hard it is to become the fastest person in the world?* I wondered. *It shouldn't be easy, and it shouldn't happen every day. And it certainly shouldn't happen just because you're wearing the right outfit.*

I resented the super suit and the effect it had, so deeply I couldn't even express it. It just seemed incredibly unfair. It made me feel like the sport I loved had been corrupted, in a way I had never seen before.

I was despondent in Rome. More than anything, I was burnt out. The suits were just another thing that felt out of my control. I took home a bronze medal in the 100-metre freestyle, a silver in the 4x100-metre medley relay and a bronze in the 4x100-metre freestyle relay, which was barely better than I had achieved six years earlier in Barcelona. Things were slipping backwards, it seemed, slowly but surely. Maybe I had made a mistake trying to keep my career afloat. This dream I had—*I will finish a champion*—was slipping through my fingers.

I sat in a corridor with Luke, in the hotel where the Australian team was staying, and we talked for a solid hour about my career and where we had ended up. I told him that I was ready to retire, and he understood. He could see how emotionally depleted I was—by the suits, by Sydney, by everything. He backed me, like he always did. I would swim at the Australian Short Course Championships, which had always been my greatest arena, and that would provide me with the high I needed to help me leave the sport with my pride intact. I wanted to feel great about swimming again before I said goodbye.

At the Short Course Championships in August 2009, I broke the world record in the 100-metre freestyle. I swam 51.01, my personal best. It was an amazing moment, and I had no regrets. I was doubly sure coming out of that achievement that it was time to retire. Unfortunately, I couldn't announce it. My management team decided that it was better for me in terms of my career prospects to be retiring *to* something. If I had a post-swimming career lined up, I had a story to tell that would make me a more attractive candidate for media and sponsorship opportunities that might arise in the future. I knew they meant well, and they had experience with this sort of thing; as well, athletes who just retired and disappeared into oblivion often seemed to struggle with mental health, in addition to being forgotten in the public sphere. My managers just wanted me to delay my announcement until they'd found me a job outside swimming.

If it were up to me, I would have just ripped the bandaid off. Instead, I was left in this nowhere place, with nothing meaningful to do, in a city I didn't like. And the only meaningful decision I made in the next few months was that I wasn't going to exercise anymore. No more punishing routines at the pool, no more gruelling gym sessions, no more hammering, sweaty spin cycles on the exercise bike. Not even a daily run or a weekly swim at the local pool. I had been training virtually nonstop for ten years, 35 hours a week, 48 weeks a year, and I just didn't want a bar of it anymore. I was so sick of it all.

Luke was working from home and I was home all the time, so we were on top of each other at a time when I felt completely hollowed out and deflated. He worked in his office and I sat on the couch, eating as much as I had when I was training without recognising that my body didn't need the fuel. I'd start the day with four pieces of toast and two eggs, eat two huge rolls for lunch and then three bowls of spaghetti for dinner. I was so accustomed to eating before I got hungry as an athlete, to keep all of the circuitry pumping, that I didn't really understand what hunger or satiety felt like. The reality was I was eating far too much, and I gained weight as a result. The funny thing is, I didn't care. I was tired, but not physically tired. I just slipped into a weird limbo where nothing really mattered.

My retirement was announced late in 2009, along with the news that I had landed a job with Channel 10 in early 2010 as a reporter for *Sports Tonight*. I had no qualifications, no experience and no mentor on the job; I was just a 24-year-old woman who had spent most of her life soaked in chlorine, who was suddenly expected to produce feature segments. However burnt out I felt after Rome, however frustrated I was in the holding pattern that came afterwards, it was nothing compared to the cold shock of feeling utterly out of my depth at this new three-day-a-week role. I didn't connect with the job, so I wasn't willing to apply myself to get better at it; the sum total of the experience was that I felt terrible about myself and my life. The best thing I can say about the job is that it didn't last long: the network went through a cost-cutting phase and I was finished just as abruptly as I had started.

I was lost. I didn't realise how much of my identity had been tied up in swimming. I thought I'd done a good job of being more than just Olympic Gold Medallist Libby Trickett. I had studied, I had a husband, I had friends and family. There was so much to my life outside of the pool— right? But the further I drifted from the routine, from the performance, from the demands and expectations, the more I realised that it was the whole anchor of my being. I mean, of course it was—swimming had consumed most of the hours of my life—but I hadn't pictured what life would be like when it didn't. *Who am I now? What are my goals? Who do I want to be? How do I value myself? And what on earth do I talk to people about?*

Everything felt like it was crumbling around me. To make matters worse, things with Luke had got very bad. We'd just stopped having fun together. It was like a fog had fallen over our relationship, and when we weren't bickering about something or other, we were cold and distant, like two strangers who were struggling along separate paths.

Every part of our lives was unwinding, and our love for each other followed suit. We frustrated each other, and we were unhappy. Nothing was working the way that it should.

I don't exactly know how my teenage sweetheart became so alien to me, but we got to the point, a year after Rome, when I just didn't see a future for us anymore. I couldn't imagine my life without Luke, but I couldn't see how we could move forward. One night I sat on the edge of our bed and said, 'I need you to leave.'

In September 2010, Luke moved out of our rental house in Lilyfield and back in with his parents. I was left completely alone. And I felt completely numb.

Chapter Eight

2016

'You can't pour from an empty cup.'

—Unknown

It's very easy to look like you're fine, to look like you're coping, when you're actually falling to pieces. You can't ever really know what is going on for someone else. When things with Poppy are at their worst, I do a couple of TV spots for Channel 7 and there are publicity shots in which I'm grinning from ear to ear. I cannot and will not let the world know how I am collapsing inside. I'm meant to be a champion. It has been my job to be the best—it's my value, my brand, isn't it? I'm supposed to be brilliant, and fit and healthy, and post-natal depression has no place in that story. But that's part of what is keeping me trapped. My life changes the minute I ask for help.

Sitting in the car outside the gym, I wait until the weeping subsides and then I pick up the phone and call Luke, and he can hear immediately that something is different—that I am different. 'I'm not okay,' I cry. 'I can't do this.' The love and concern in Luke's voice is palpable. He tells me we're going to get some help and that everything *will* be okay. He's been waiting and wanting so badly to try to make things better for us, and he's desperately concerned for me and Poppy, but I can also hear the slight edge of relief in his voice.

I feel the relief too. For some reason, I can now see that things are not normal. I'm not just weak or a shitty mother, I'm having a genuine psychological crisis, and it's not my fault. It's not my fault. The instant I recognise this, I feel more in control. I know instinctively that if I can identify the problem, I have a much better chance of fighting it.

That afternoon, I call my GP and make an appointment to see him the following day. I'm every bit as tired and devastated as I was in the morning, but just the act of reaching out has shifted some weight inside me. It feels like there is a possibility for something to change, and it stirs some small reserve of hope in my mind. I need to hold on to that sliver of hope, to find my way out of the dark.

Mum is taking care of Poppy during my appointment. I struggle to concentrate when I'm with my baby and I know that this needs my full attention, but it was really hard to admit to my mother that I was having such a difficult time.

I'm just so grateful that she is there to help me. I don't know what I'd do without her. We don't talk about it in much depth, because my mother is not what you'd call talkative. She likes to be there, to be helpful.

Sitting opposite my doctor, talking about how bad things have got, is one of the most confronting and yet comforting experiences of my life. I'm fairly new to Dr Michael Clem, but he is incredibly attentive and thorough. I get the sense that he really cares about his patients. I know that I've been through many episodes of depression. Of course, my swimming career was intense and sometimes traumatic, and it often felt like the world was caving in on me when things didn't go to plan. When Luke and I separated, I saw a psychologist and considered going on antidepressants, and since I stopped swimming there have been so many moments when I've felt unhappy, but I know that this is something else. This is not something that will pass by itself. And it feels like so much more is hingeing on this moment. I still feel that deep responsibility to protect and nurture Poppy. It's my duty to try to get better, not just for myself but for her. For Poppy it is even more important.

Dr Clem gives me a diagnostic test—a series of questions about how I'm sleeping, how I'm eating, how I'm feeling and how I'm thinking—that gives a measure of how a person is coping psychologically. When we're done, he is unequivocal. 'It's clear that you have postnatal depression,' he says. 'So let's get you some help.' He reassures me that what I'm going through, while genuinely awful, is also really common. I'm not completely bonkers, and I'm not a failure—I am just going through something that so many women face, and there are things he can do to help.

He draws up a mental-health care plan for me, which gives me access to the services of a psychologist, and we talk about whether or not medication is appropriate right now. We decide that it isn't, but we know that we can go there if we need to. Dr Clem emphasises how important it is for me to be open and honest with my family and friends, to ask for support when I need it without feeling ashamed. And he stresses that sleep is the main thing that is going to improve my situation, so getting some assistance with Poppy's sleep patterns should be a top priority. I know he's right. I also know the journey is going to be a long one, but I leave the doctor's office feeling like I have taken my first step in the right direction.

I make an appointment with Georgia Ridler, the psychologist I have seen throughout my sports career. Although she specialises in sports psychology, she also has a broader practice, and I've developed a great relationship with her over the years. She was there for me when I needed to cultivate a peak-performance mindset. She was there for me when I left swimming and was struggling with the transition to normal life. She's the only person I want to see now. I never thought I would be coming to Georgia with something like postnatal depression, but I know that I can trust her. I also know she understands me, and she understands all the baggage I've been carrying around all these years that is no doubt having an impact on how I feel.

Every new conversation I have with someone about my feelings makes them a little easier to bear. The shame lessens a little and my resolve strengthens a fraction. Most importantly, there is a process now that I am supposed to follow. Georgia also puts decent sleep at the top of the list of things that I need to help me get better. It's not like I haven't understood that being overtired has been the key driver of this emotional instability, and of course that's what Luke has been saying all along, but it's different when two health professionals tell you that sleep has to be your main priority. It's almost like they have given me permission to let go of the self-judgement and shame that I've been carrying because of my obsession with attachment parenting. They make it clear that if I don't start getting decent sleep, I will only be hurting myself and my baby.

Georgia and Dr Clem also talk to me about needing time to myself. They want me to organise blocks of time where Poppy is with Mum, or to consider a day of childcare each week so I can get some breathing space to rest and recover. I'm a stay-at-home mum, so I never would have considered childcare as an option, and it's both confronting and a revelation to have two healthcare professionals tell me I should think about it. Again, it feels like they are giving me permission to do something that I would have been far too ashamed to do otherwise, even if it had occurred to me, which it hadn't.

The other crucial part of the recovery plan—something that Georgia in particular knows is especially important for me—is to get regular exercise. I can't rely on Mums and Bubs at the gym, I need to prioritise finding time alone to get my body moving, because my physical wellbeing is very closely connected to my emotional wellbeing. If I push my body, get the blood pumping and the endorphins flowing, I know that I will be working the stress and grief out of my system.

Most of all, though, I need sleep. So many of my dark thoughts, so much of my behaviour, is heavily entwined with the fact that I haven't slept properly in over nine months. This is the message I get over and over again from my doctors, and it's the number-one thing I have to change. When I get home from my appointment with Georgia, I google the number for Katie Forsythe, the baby sleep consultant. After a huge breath I pick up the phone, and take another step towards being okay.

About a week later, Katie comes to spend the night with us, to observe how Poppy and I function and see what we can change. She is such a dream of a person—she puts me at ease immediately with her warmth and her jokes and her general kindness. I feel so safe in her hands. There is steel in there too, which is what I need. She won't tolerate me saying that I'm a terrible mother because my baby won't sleep, and she doesn't let me take the blame for where we have ended up.

'I've obviously created this situation,' I fret.

'No,' Katie replies. 'Some babies sleep and some babies don't, and that's just how it is. Certainly, things are exacerbated by different behaviours, but everything you've done so far, you've done to try and help your child. You're not a bad person for feeding your baby to sleep, and you're not a bad person for rocking your baby to sleep—you were just trying to see what would work. And that is totally okay.'

Katie has a favourite expression and she uses it a lot: *If it's not a problem for you, it's not a problem.* Her philosophy is that there is no one single way to be a good mother, so you need to do your best and focus on whatever works for you. There's nothing wrong with rocking your baby to sleep, but if you're doing it for two hours every night, in the middle of the night, and it's making you even more sleep-deprived and crazy, then you might need to reconsider it.

Katie is with us from the early evening, observing our routine and going over the options for sleep training that we might want to consider. There are two main options, one of which involves sitting next to the baby and soothing them when they cry, but moving a little bit further away each night until eventually you're sitting just outside the door. The other option she suggests is timed retreat, which is a form of controlled crying. There is a big distinction between controlled crying and crying it out, I discover. Crying it out involves just leaving the child to cry themselves to sleep, which just seems too traumatic to me—*all that stress, no, it's definitely not for me.* And Katie doesn't advocate it anyway. Controlled crying, or timed retreat, involves leaving the baby to cry for short intervals, then coming back in to touch them, kiss them and reassure them that you are still around before leaving the room again. Each time you leave the room, you stay away for a little longer, and each night those intervals get further and further apart. You are never that far away, and your baby is never left for so long that that wailing hysteria sets in.

It hurts to leave my baby to cry. It hurts not to take her in my arms and try to soothe her, but Katie is such a calm and reassuring presence for me that we make it through the night being faithful to her system. And Poppy sleeps about eleven hours altogether, which by morning seems like some kind of miracle. She wakes up once during the night, but only for a couple of minutes, and I get the longest stretch of sleep I've had in literally nine months, which is so stunning to my body that it feels like I have jet lag. Coupled with this slightly drunk feeling, the fact that Katie's system worked is unbelievable to me. On the one hand, it goes against my natural instincts to let my baby cry, but to see results so quickly is just mind-boggling. And I slept. *I slept!* I am absolutely amazed.

Katie explains that we all have natural sleep cycles, and certain senses that are activated when our sleep cycle comes to an end. 'Very likely, when you're co-sleeping with Poppy, her sense of touch is triggered when she begins to wake up. She's gone to sleep with a nipple in her mouth and it's missing when she stirs. She's obviously very alert to that sensation and to the change that she feels. But when she goes to sleep without the nipple in her mouth, her body isn't sensing a change so it's much easier for her to relax back into sleep.'

The second night, when it's just me and Luke doing the same routine at bedtime, Poppy goes down by herself and sleeps the entire night through.

What I've come to understand is that motherhood isn't a competition. It's not that women are trying to outdo each other, it's just that everyone thinks they might know better. Everyone seems to think that their own experience is the same as that of other women. I know that not every woman would have the same reaction that I am having to sleep deprivation. I know that some women would cope much better than I am coping. I hear of women who haven't slept through in two or three years, and I am utterly astounded. These women who can work, and maintain their relationships, and be nice to their family, and function in the world, on month after month of broken sleep are incredible. I applaud them, I guess, but that just isn't me.

My sister co-slept with all her children, and did it for a very long time. When I decide to see Katie, I sense that my sister is disappointed in me, and I resent her for it—it makes me feel worse and contributes to my sense of guilt and of failure—and that in turn causes a rift. But all I can do right now is deal with my own reality and try to make the best decision for my family.

I'm starting to understand that every family experiences different things at different stages. If your baby is waking three times a night and you're happy to feed them and put them back to sleep, cool, that's fine, you don't have to do sleep training. If you're co-sleeping and the baby is sleeping, and you're sleeping, and you're getting time to yourself and feeling refreshed and re-energised in the morning, it's not a problem. But if your baby is waking constantly during the night and you're struggling, there are things you can do to create a better environment, to teach the baby how to resettle and go back to sleep.

It takes me a long time to feel comfortable telling people that we sleep-trained Poppy, because I still feel the residual shame, and I discover that there are plenty of people in the world who are happy to judge you without having walked in your shoes. It's a pity we do this to each other, especially as women. It's a pity we don't have more compassion for what other mothers might be going through.

Within two weeks of sleep training, I feel like a new person. Within two weeks, we also find a position for Poppy in childcare—a near miracle in the early-childhood world. The fact that my schedule is completely flexible helps a lot, of course, and when they offer us Mondays we gratefully accept. I take Poppy in the following week. Walking away and leaving her there nearly breaks my heart, and I last about an hour at home before I go back to pick her up. The following week, we make it to two hours, and we slowly build from there. At first, Poppy seems completely unfazed when I leave, but I think it's because she hasn't figured out what's going on. By the third or fourth week, she wails miserably when I drop her off, but the staff assure me she's happy as a pig in mud for the rest of the day.

I struggle initially with the guilt, and spend a few lonely Monday mornings sitting on the couch feeling dejected. But eventually it occurs to me that I'm only wasting my time. This downtime is for Poppy as much as it is for me, because she needs me to be healthy and strong emotionally. And there is absolutely no point sitting around feeling miserable when I'm supposed to be caring for myself and relaxing. If I'm going to do this, I might as well do it properly.

It's barely one day a week. It's just a few hours really, because generally I drop Pops off at 9 a.m. and pick her up again at 2 p.m. But those hours are mine, completely guilt-free. I can get my nails done or get a massage or go and sit in a cafe with friends. I can lie on the couch and sleep, or binge-watch Netflix—anything I feel like doing. The important thing from a mental health point of view is feeling like I have control over my own time, that I'm not trapped in this hamster wheel of feeds, naps and nappy changes.

Instinctively, I want to call it selfishness, but with guidance from Georgia and Dr Clem, I tell myself that that's not what it's about. When I let myself get to the point of burnout, I was a terrible person—short-tempered, angry and emotionally dysfunctional. I have to take the time to nourish myself and to refill the well of love and calm inside of me, so that I have something to give.

A huge part of my new routine is about exercise. At the peak of Poppy's sleeping troubles, I'd be lucky if I got to the gym once a week. I was too tired, it wasn't a priority, I dreaded the car ride, what was the point . . . Even knowing how much better I would feel after some exercise, I just couldn't motivate myself half the time. This has to change. I know that when I exercise I get completely out of my head and am completely present in my body, and that feeling is incredibly powerful for me. It's really centring and peaceful. I've never thought about it in these terms, but it is a kind of mindfulness. It's a form of meditation that works for me, which is something I sorely need. I need to get back in the water.

Getting back in the pool always feels like returning home. The weightlessness, that feeling that I am gliding along the surface, is my happiest place. I love the sound of the water rushing past my ears and the feeling of the sun on my arms. I love stretching every muscle through freestyle and backstroke, from my core through my feet and the tips of my fingers. I start making more time to swim again, for the exercise and the endorphins, but the measured lengths up and down the pool also let my body breathe. I have a ritual at the end of every session where I swim most of 100 metres completely underwater. There is a special silence under there that makes my heart calm. After I've finished, I like to float on my back and gaze up at the sky, looking for patterns in the clouds. It doesn't take more than half an hour a week, but this habit helps me to heal.

Through this period, Luke is incredible. He's not the most romantic guy, he's not always very expressive or communicative, and he's not especially emotionally intuitive, but when he gets it, he gets it. And he really gets this. Our usual dynamic of driving and challenging each other to do better and be better has shifted, and he has nothing but loving support for me right now. I know he's grateful for the guidance we've had from others, and because (like me) he is a very process-oriented person, he has put his faith in the process. Here are the tools—this is how we fix it. He never questions the things I need to get through, or gives any hint of resentment. I'm lucky he's on my team; I feel blessed to have him in my life.

As I get stronger and emerge from my depression—which takes months, not days—I start to experience moments of pure joy with Poppy that I haven't felt for a very long time. The heavy blanket that smothered my love for her, the fog that made me feel so disconnected and detached from the sweet, precious gift that she is, slowly starts to lift. And it's only when I'm on the other side that I realise how much I was missing. When I was sick, I saw logically that she was adorable and thought logically that she was mine, but I didn't feel it with my whole heart—I didn't know it was missing. Once the fog starts to clear, the sunlight pours in, and my daughter becomes my little miracle again, and also just an average kid.

Our new normal is normal—dirty nappies, teething, bedtime stories, tantrums. *No, you can't have a fifth bottle of milk today. No, you can't watch another hour of* Paw Patrol. *Yes, we can go to the park after lunch. Yes, Daddy will be home for dinner.* There are finger paintings and dress-ups and birthday parties to attend. I'm tired, but it's a normal kind of tired, and I feel stronger than I've ever been. My life as a mum is hard work, fun, funny, frustrating and incredible. It's exactly like it should be.

2010

'When I let go of what I am, I become what
I might be. When I let go of what I have,
I receive what I need.'

—*Tao Te Ching*

I just couldn't see how Luke and I could get back to the
way we had once been. We'd been taking each other for
granted for so long, treating each other badly, and it had
tainted our relationship so much that it seemed unlikely we
would ever recover. But still, I couldn't let him go. It felt
like I was missing a limb. What saved us was that we were
both willing to work on ourselves, separately. We recognised
that we weren't working as a couple, but that was primarily
because we were both pretty messed up at that stage: we had
to sort out our own issues before we could consider how to

reconnect with each other. The love we had was always there, but it was buried underneath responsibilities, stress, disappointment, frustration, anxiety, depression and dislocation. We had to take responsibility for our own broken feelings before we looked at each other.

Luke and I lived apart for six months, the second half of 2010. During that time, we saw counsellors separately, and went to couples counselling together. Part of the process for both of us was navigating what it meant to grow up together—to understand how much people change from their late teens to their mid-twenties—and to recognise that while we had been together, we had been on separate journeys of learning and discovery. When we got together, Luke and I both still had to navigate the transition to adulthood, which is challenging for everyone. We were both trying to figure out who we were and what we wanted to be, and at the same time trying to work together on major life plans and decisions. The biggest problem we had, ultimately, was that we'd stopped having fun together. We'd become so consumed by our own personal shit that we had stopped enjoying ourselves and each other. And that's where the connection died.

While Luke and I gingerly navigated the broken pieces of our relationship, I continued to feel lost. I had no real career prospects, no sense of direction, and an overwhelming feeling that I had taken a wrong turn at some point and needed to get back to my life's true path. The only way that I could see myself not being lost was to go back to swimming. I needed an anchor point, a foundation for my life, and the only place I knew I could find it was in the water. It was all I had ever known. I knew the structure, I knew the routine, and I knew that it would give me a goal to work towards, to combat this feeling that I was just floating in space.

When I'd made it to the top level of the sport, I had dreamed of making it to three Olympic Games. This was something few athletes had managed to do, and had become a marker of swimming achievement. For me, life had got in the way—I had challenges and disappointments, and ultimately I'd been distracted from that goal. And I regretted it, after I retired, because it felt like unfinished business. If I went back to swimming, I decided, I would aim for the London Olympics in 2012. That was reason enough, but it wasn't the main reason. More than anything, I just wanted to find myself again. Libby the swimmer knew what to do. Libby the swimmer was in control; she could set goals and work towards them. It gave me a sense of value.

I felt no sense of embarrassment or awkwardness about the fact that I was coming out of retirement so soon after I'd quit. A number of swimmers around that time were doing the same thing, so it wasn't even particularly unusual. I knew I might fail, but I couldn't not do it. Even if people judged me, or if they were sceptical, the feeling of centredness I got just from making the decision told me that it was the right path. And Stolly was incredibly supportive and pleased when I went to him. He welcomed me with open arms.

So, towards the end of 2010, I went back to Stolly's team and started training again—and it immediately became apparent that I was grossly out of shape. I had treated my body with disregard for a year, I had gained ten kilos, and I was way off my game. As soon as I got back in the water I had doubts that I could achieve what I wanted to in the sport, but the feeling was oddly galvanising for me. I was programmed to face my doubts and my shortcomings in the pool, and to work systematically to overcome them; I had years of experience doing just that. It was in the real world I struggled, because I didn't know what I needed to do.

I started slowly and clawed my way back—four training sessions a week, then six sessions, and finally up to nine; then came the gym sessions, the cardio, the core. It wasn't pretty. I was very sore and very tired for what felt like a long time, but the physical punishment was also a comfort to me, because every muscle ache meant I was getting stronger. There was discussion around my physical shape, but Stolly was very kind about it. He never said I was fat or implied that I couldn't get back to where I'd been before, although it was as plain as day that I was miles off my peak. Stolly was nothing but encouraging and optimistic, which was just what I needed.

Unfortunately, nothing about the social environment in Stolly's team had changed, in that I still felt like a square peg in a round hole. But I worked as hard as I could in the pool, and outside of it I continued to go to counselling and talk about a future with Luke. In retrospect, I can see that they were all tentative steps, a slow sharpening of focus. I was coming out of the fog, feeling stronger and more confident every week, but definitely still figuring things out.

Luke and I spent Christmas together, on a driving holiday between Brisbane and Sydney, which turned out to be a terrible idea. We're weren't campers—we didn't even realise that you had to book camping spots, so we spent more than one night 'camping' on the side of the road. But it was a really fun experience, which was the whole idea. Through our counselling, we had decided that it was crucial for us to start enjoying each other again, and we had started dating regularly, like two young people in love. It was a bit odd going to Luna Park and the movies with a man I was already married to, but we'd both made a commitment to start again, and we both really meant it. Each of us understood that the only way we could move forward was to let go of the past, and we did it. We found the lightness in our love again. We made each other laugh.

In February 2011 I went with Stolly and the squad to an altitude training camp in Mexico, where the thin atmosphere forces your body to process air more efficiently, creating big fat blood cells that have a greater capacity to carry oxygen around your body. We were going to be there for several weeks, and I found that I was really reluctant to be away from

Luke during that time. We were still living apart, but increasingly I felt like it wasn't right anymore. It didn't help that the days were pretty boring and repetitive, and the nights were very low-key. Also, my body didn't seem to be responding the way the others did. I never really felt breathless, which was supposed to be an indicator that the altitude training might be working, but we did a few hikes and I did cardio workouts every day to try to shift the weight that I'd put on in retirement. Mostly I thought very hard about the life I wanted when I got home. Luke and I were in a really good place—we were talking every day. I was absolutely sure that I wanted to be with him, so one night when we spoke I asked him to move back in with me when I got home. He didn't hesitate because he felt the same way; we were a team again.

When Luke and I decided to get back together, it was a serious and solid commitment—no hesitation and no looking back. We started looking for a house to buy in Sydney, but quickly realised that it just wasn't the city for us. Nothing about the city had clicked. We hadn't taken the time to stop and reflect on where we actually wanted to be, but the minute we started looking at Sydney house prices, it was like a lightbulb flicked on over our heads. We didn't want to pay an exorbitant price to live in a city we hated. We wanted to move back to Brisbane—to our family, friends and a lifestyle we loved. I think Stolly was disappointed in my decision, but on some level he'd probably anticipated it. I think he knew I wasn't entirely happy in the squad, so he was very gracious about me leaving.

Once the choice was made, we snapped into action. Within a month, Luke and I were back home. To try to save money, we moved into a one-room hut that belonged to some very good friends of ours, and quickly found that living on top of each other was a crazy idea. We had three dogs, a leaky toilet and all our belongings jammed into a very small space, but our intention was to buy some land and build a home, so the cheap rent was extremely helpful.

Immediately after we'd settled in, I went back to train with Stephan. He welcomed me back to his squad as easily as he'd let me go, and it was up to me to deal with the fact that I would be training alongside Jess. But with everything that had happened over the preceding year, I was in a completely different place and the prospect bothered me far less. The squad was different, full of young and unfamiliar faces, but I was comfortable with that too. More than anything, I wanted to work with the coach who knew me best and would drive me hardest to succeed.

But Stephan had changed too in the time that I was away—he seemed nowhere near as hardcore as he used to be. It felt like he had backed off from the ferocious drive that put us both on the map. He had been such an intense character, driving people, riding them, constantly pushing them beyond what they believed they were capable of, and I suspect he was just a little burnt out. It took so much energy to build a champion.

Having said that, I still found Stephan's training regime far more punishing than Stolly's. I really only began to realise how out of shape I was when I went back to Brisbane, because his style of training was so much more aggressive. At my peak with Stephan, I would easily complete a 100-metre kick cycle in under two minutes, with only the power in my legs. I just couldn't make it when I went back—I couldn't even come close. There was nothing in the tank. I didn't have the strength or the aerobic fitness, and I began to seriously doubt whether I could ever make it back. *Did I actually do competitive swimming?* I wondered. *Was I actually an Olympic champion at some point? Maybe I just dreamed the whole thing . . .*

I was now a mature athlete, too, which made everything that much harder. Gone were the days when I could just think about losing millimetres of skinfold and off it came. My metabolism had changed, my body was older and didn't respond as quickly as it once had. It felt like it wasn't responding at all, to be honest, but in reality it was just happening more slowly. I did the work and it happened. I recognised that I was now a different athlete and made some necessary changes, like learning about and focusing on my nutrition. I followed a diet plan for the first time in my career. It occurred to me that if I'd actually followed the recommended nutrition plan in my younger years, I might have been an even better athlete.

I made steady improvement, creeping back into fighting form, but just as I felt like I was getting back into my stride, a wrist injury pulled me out of training. I developed a pocket of fluid called a ganglion in my right wrist, a tiny internal bubble that created a huge amount of pain and required surgery, which kept me away from the 2011 World Championship trials. At the same time, I developed a hand condition called De Quervain syndrome in my left wrist, which made it hard to manoeuvre my thumb until I had a couple of cortisone injections.

My frustration was immense—I'd never had to deal with injuries before—but on some level I understood that it was part and parcel of being a slightly older swimmer. In Sydney I had trained with Eamon Sullivan, who had suffered what seemed like a thousand injuries and just kept going. He somehow managed to break his heel while jumping into the pool in Mexico, and just kept swimming.

I had plenty of role models to guide me through. I knew my body was more vulnerable, but I was also confident that I could and would get stronger, because that's what happens to female sprinters—their power increases in the mid to late twenties. I had faith that my body would do the same. It was inevitable that there would be challenges with my comeback, but I had so much clarity and focus, and purpose, that nothing felt insurmountable. It felt like I had control over my life again. I had a sense of direction, which empowered me to believe that I would develop some clarity about what I wanted to do with my life in a broader sense—though, ironically, in that intense training regime, you really have no time to think about anything else.

I was extremely disappointed to miss the World Championships, because I felt like I needed the opportunity to see where I was at and experience an elite-level competition ahead of the London Games. I did make it to the World Cup tour, swimming three short-course meets in the Asia Pacific leg. My results weren't great, which again was frustrating. I was confronted with the reality that I might not make it to London, or make it in the capacity that I wanted to, which was to compete in individual races. But that only made me more determined to improve.

All this happened under the spotlight of media attention. It was an awkward time for the sport, because some other swimmers and I—dubbed 'the comeback kids'—were receiving financial support from Swimming Australia, and there was conjecture in the media and among other athletes about whether we had earned it, when we hadn't acquitted ourselves particularly well on the international scene and I wasn't part of the World Championship team. There were some loud voices suggesting we shouldn't receive any funding at all under those circumstances.

My reaction to this was fairly composed, which I think was a sign of my growing maturity. Instead of collapsing into self-doubt and a sense of unworthiness, I reflected on the situation and tried to back myself. I know I had done some great things for Australian swimming in the past, and it was my full and passionate intention to do great things for the sport again. I didn't think I had anything to apologise for. Geoff Huegill, Michael Klim and Ian Thorpe were also in the crosshairs, but when those three came out of retirement, they created a huge buzz that made people tune into swimming again. It wasn't even about how they performed— the huge media attention and public interest they generated had value in and of itself.

Luke was my rock through all of this. After we made the commitment to each other, our relationship went to a new level. We worked together, nurtured each other and always had each other's back. It made every challenge I had in the water that much more bearable, because he supported me even more than he ever had before. I was battling my body, constantly under some kind of stress, but nothing was unmanageable this time around. I was where I was supposed to be, with the man I was supposed to be with, and I had faith that everything would be okay.

Chapter Nine

2017

'What if I fall? Oh, but my darling, what if you fly?'

—Erin Hanson

My deterioration into mental illness was slow and subtle, and my recovery is slow and subtle too. There is no magic bullet. There is no day when I wake up and think, *Fantastic, I'm cured!* I still feel a lingering sense of failure, a lingering sense of unworthiness, a lingering sense of frustration that I can't control every outcome, but they become softer and more manageable with every day that passes. The dark thoughts start to ebb away until I realise one day that I haven't had one for a very long time.

During my recovery, we move from the house we own in Seven Hills to a rental property in New Farm. I realised that I was feeling incredibly claustrophobic and cut off from the world in the old house. I needed to be close to a park and cafes, to have the outside world within walking distance. Poppy is such a high-energy toddler, and when she starts walking, at around eleven months, I want to make sure she has the space to move and climb. We need the green, open places and river walks that New Farm has to offer, and our new house is closer to Poppy's childcare, which makes life easier as well. Moving house also helps me to move the emotional weight inside of me. Some part of it is left behind at the old place; New Farm helps me heal.

Talking to my friends also helps. I have a group Messenger chat with my closest girlfriends, and I tell them that we worked with Katie to help Poppy to sleep. There were obviously indications before that moment that my life wasn't smooth sailing, but I think this is the moment I really let my friends in, and let them know how dark things had become for me. At first I am reluctant to use the words 'postnatal depression', because I don't always like labelling things. People assume that if you have depression you have to be medicated, which is absolutely essential for some people, but that hasn't been the case for me. I want them to understand but not judge me, so I've been a little ginger in my approach, but now I've started to think that labels can actually make things easier to talk about. Instead of feeling ashamed about having a mental illness, I want to feel more comfortable naming it and talking about it. I want my friends and family to understand that depression and mental illness exist on a spectrum: some days are bad, but some days are really great, and everyone's experience is very different.

Of course, when I have the courage to be really honest with my friends, their true colours shine through. They're compassionate, loving people. I don't feel judged. I feel embraced, even by those women who haven't had the same experience because their babies were seemingly easier or their psychological disposition is different to mine. I know the world is full of women who have children and cope just fine with it, but that wasn't me, and that wasn't my fault. I'm not deficient or broken or bad because I had postnatal depression, nor is any other woman who suffers through it.

For me, Poppy's sleep deprivation was a trigger, and probably changed things physiologically and psychologically in my body. For others, a traumatic birth could be the trigger, or the flood of hormones that rushes through our bodies during pregnancy, or maybe pre-existing mental-health conditions that are aggravated by the challenges of caring for a newborn baby. I've been reading a lot about it recently, and my eyes are wide open now. It helps me to talk about it, and my friends are ready and willing to listen. 'You're doing pretty well, all things considered,' a girlfriend tells me, which is really nice to hear.

I go back to work just after we move house. I'd started back at Megaport in a marketing and events role just before I got pregnant with Poppy, and had extended my maternity leave because of the struggles we'd had, but Luke and I are still not fully recovered from our financial troubles and I need to be working. It's only three days a week, which is manageable, and I actually think it's helping with my recovery to have some part of my identity that is not just being a mother. I massively appreciate the social connection—having adult conversations is a refreshing change of pace.

It's challenging, of course. Actually, that's an understatement—it's fucking hard being a working mother, and there is a whole different category of guilt associated with having to leave work because your child is sick, or skipping out on a meeting because you have to pick them up from childcare. But I'm lucky to be working with supportive people; they've been understanding the whole way through this process. When Poppy was six months old and I was in the depths of despair, I had to go to my team at Megaport and tell them that I just wasn't ready to come back. The heads of the parent company are American, and just don't have the cultural grounding to understand what extended maternity leave is. They also don't have children. I think it might have been the first time that mental-health issues had been discussed so openly with them as well, but to their credit they took everything I said on board and told me to take all the time I needed. I will be eternally grateful for that. If they had demanded that I go back to work at six months, I would have been forced to quit, which would have created more financial stress at exactly the wrong time.

Now that I'm back, and feeling better, I'm in a good groove. I am so much better suited to the new role at Megaport, which is focused on event planning and creating marketing collateral. I organise meet-ups and events between prospective clients and our sales team, and coordinate Megaport's involvement at tradeshows and conferences. It's extraordinary how much more capable and confident I feel in this role, purely because I'm better suited to it. I don't have to know my way around the intimate corners of a groundbreaking yet niche technology. I don't have to generate leads and cold-call people to pitch them a product I barely understand. Marketing and events feels so simple by comparison, with very clear processes and outcomes, though the indicators of success are nowhere near as brutal. It's interesting to me that while I wanted to be the best as a swimmer—nothing but the best—I have zero drive to be the best at sales, which in a way is equally precise and measurable. On the other hand, the process of preparing for an event—following the process, doing the work and then having everything come together on the day—feels very familiar.

What I've learned this time around is that I don't suck. I didn't suck the first time I worked at Megaport either, I was just not the right fit for the job. People throw that expression around a lot—*not the right fit*—but I think it's a very useful way to understand the world and your place in it. No one is going to be great at everything—I'm certainly not—but I am good at some things. My current role at Megaport is good because it utilises the skills that I have. When I know what I'm doing and I understand the process, I can work hard, I can focus, I can persevere; all of the things that helped me succeed as an athlete are actually transferrable skills. I work well in a team environment too. I have a bit of experience there.

The only challenge for me, which affects my level of commitment to the job and probably means I am not a really extraordinary employee, is that I'm not actually passionate about technology. I'm also very clear that I don't want to work in an office job long-term—my body just isn't geared for it. But I don't know what I want to do instead. I can feel an energy building inside me that wants an outlet, but I'm not sure what to do with it yet. I'm just conscious that it's there.

I still have the occasional TV gig. I've been on the *Daily Edition* and the *Morning Show* on Channel 7 several times since Poppy was born, usually just as 'former Olympic champion Libby Trickett, dropping in to say hello'. I've been posting fairly open and honest accounts of what I've been going through on social media, minus the seriously dark stuff, so my TV appearances have been geared around the challenges of being a mother.

At seven months, Poppy came on air with me: she bawled the entire time, tried to crawl off the desk and grabbed at everything within reach, but I remained sunny and seemingly lucid about how tricky it is to be a mum, which is kind of hilarious. It is strange, though, to see how broadly I could smile on TV when my private life was crumbling. That's the people pleaser in me again: not wanting to be too vulnerable, not wanting to make anyone feel uncomfortable, being honest without being entirely true. It's also a coping mechanism for me to make light of things, and that's exactly what I was doing. It was the best I could do at the time. Behind the scenes, I was tearing myself to shreds.

It's not until Poppy is about twelve months old that I really open up in public about how bad things were, about my depression and my rock bottom. I talk about those things publicly when I'm strong enough to do it. I talk about it because I think it's important to acknowledge what happened, because I want other women going through similar things to know that they're not alone, and because I want to forgive myself. I'm still working on that. I want to move forward, and that means I can't carry the grief and guilt about what happened around with me every day. But I do think it's good to pick it up and look at it every now and then, to remind myself how far I've come.

While all this is going on, I'm still in the public eye, and still searching for that next career move that will broaden my world a little more. I get a call from a producer at the Southern Cross Austereo radio network, who tells me there's an opportunity coming up—he's wondering if I'd like to audition for the new Triple M drive-time show in Brisbane. A veteran radio guy called Luke Bradnam is going to anchor the team, and they need to find the right co-hosts to bounce off his energy. I've had a little exposure to radio over the years, and a brief maternity leave fill-in role for the then Labby, Stav and Abby show on B105, but I think it's fair to say that I'm absolutely green. Still, I jump at the chance. I love to talk, and I love to laugh. Maybe radio will become my new passion.

I do an air test with Luke in December 2017 and then absolutely nothing happens. I don't hear a peep out of Triple M for six weeks. *Must have absolutely nailed the audition*, I think, trying not to be too disappointed. They're obviously auditioning everyone under the sun and I'm just another girl in the line. It's out of my hands anyway—I know it's about on-air chemistry, and you can't force that. I thought Luke and I had it, but perhaps I'm not quite as charming as I imagined.

By mid-January, I can't bear waiting anymore so I give the producer a call to follow up, which takes quite a lot of balls on my behalf. This triggers another four or five air tests with Luke and me, with a different man in the third chair each time. There are radio presenters, comedians, former athletes and a sports commentator named Ben 'Dobbo' Dobbin, who ends up landing the job. I get the job as well, thank god, and come February I have left Megaport and started a brand-new career as a drive-time radio host.

My job is to come up with funny anecdotes about my life so that Luke, Dobbo and I can talk about them on air, which is easy enough, though it does make me look at every moment through an oddly critical lens. *Luke said something funny over dinner—is that a bite? Does the world want to hear about Poppy's toilet training? Is that funny? Is that engaging? Would that be good on air?* I resist this mindset initially, but it becomes a running joke in my team that I'm not bringing enough content, so I have to at least try to get with the program.

In the meantime, I'm feel like I'm very good at reacting to Luke and Dobbo's stories, and there's plenty of drama in our little on-air family. We have regular segments including 'World Record Wednesdays', where I attempt to break a world record. It's ridiculous fun and I am the right woman for the task, because I am as competitive as ever. I'm up for any challenge, whether it's trying to eat a record-breaking number of Ferrero Rocher chocolates in one minute (quite hard, by the way) or putting on a record-breaking number of undies (smashed it). We have team challenges, too—rifle shooting, monster truck driving, whip cracking—and I do my best at every turn. I don't always triumph, but I do have a lot of fun. The job brings out the playful, light-hearted side of my personality, which is a nice place to be after everything I've been through. My confidence goes through the roof, along with my self-esteem. It's really nice to feel like I'm good at something again.

Metro breakfast radio always seems to be the goal. If you're a career presenter and you want to reach the top of the pile, then you're aiming for a chance at that sweet breakfast spot, which always has the biggest audience. Luke, Dobbo and I get our chance maybe six months after we start broadcasting together—a two-week backfill gig while the regular hosts are on holiday. My co-hosts are over the moon, but all I can think about is how painful it will be to get up at 4 a.m. every day and still parent as well.

And, indeed, it is extremely painful. It throws my whole routine out with Poppy and absolutely kills my social life (which is virtually non-existent anyway) because getting up at 4 a.m. makes 6 p.m. look like a reasonable bedtime. It's only the smallest window of time, but it gets me thinking: *Where am I going with this?* If breakfast radio is the ultimate goal, and I don't want to do breakfast radio, what's my goal supposed to be?

If I didn't still carry around with me that lock-jawed athlete's mindset, I'd probably just decide that drive-time radio is a fine place to be and leave it at that, but I feel like I want more, or that I'm supposed to want more. My brain starts ticking over and I find myself thinking, *This is great, but what am I* really *going to do with my life?* Radio is suddenly looking like a two-to-five-year plan.

Part of the problem is that the radio gig is fun, but it doesn't feel particularly meaningful to me. I've done better on-air than I have in any other role in my post-swimming career, which is wonderful, but now that I have some kind of mojo back, I want something meatier. I have no intention of resigning—I feel competent, I'm learning things, and my income is good for me and my family—but I'm starting to think about the bigger picture. I feel like good things are coming. I don't know what they look like, exactly, but I trust that they're in my future. Sometimes you just have to leave things up to the universe and see what happens.

It's easier for me to be optimistic these days, because Poppy is now a wonderful sleeper. Most of the time she sleeps the whole way through the night, and all the horrors of that first year have faded into the background. I've come to understand that the early intense, high-need period of a child's life really is a season, and that season passes eventually. It honestly felt for a while like she would never grow and never change, and I would never sleep again, and yet here we are eighteen months later and the whole world looks different. The more Poppy grows and communicates with me, the more she talks and expresses herself, the more delightful she is to me. And we have entered a really interesting phase of her life where she is, for the most part, pretty delightful.

Driving home from childcare one day, I ask if she wants some food, and instead of burbling or nodding her head, she looks right at me and says, 'Nana.' *Oh my god!* 'You want a banana?' I ask, and she nods. *This is amazing!*

Another day, I ask her to go to the bathroom and get the hairbrush, and she does it, and I am absolutely thrilled with her. She can't say 'bathroom' or 'hairbrush', but she knows what they are—and isn't that the most *incredible* thing? My daughter is *amazing.*

I love watching her learn to jump—it's genuinely magical to me. Watching her hit all those physical milestones—crawling, walking, hopping, skipping—gives me a special thrill. And seeing her splashing in the pool is the most beautiful thing ever.

I always knew I wanted a sibling for Pops. I want her to have an ally in life, someone she always feels connected to. I also want her to have a playmate so that it's not always my responsibility to keep her entertained, and with that in mind I feel like they need to be relatively close together in age. With life feeling generally pretty wonderful now, Luke and I start talking about having another kid. We go from talking to trying to conceive in pretty short order.

From the outset, we learn that every child is different. Conceiving is so different, and so much harder, the second time around. I can't track my cycle and don't seem to be ovulating at all; everything feels out of whack. We decide to see a doctor for some reproductive assistance, and a medication called Clomid that helps stimulate ovulation is prescribed. But even with the drugs, we struggle. We don't want to get bogged down in it, so after four cycles we decide to take a break from the project. 'We're just going to focus on other things for a while,' we tell the doctor.

'That's the kind of talk that gets you pregnant,' he laughs.

Within a few weeks, we do a test and discover that he's right.

I'm nervous, but I feel so much more prepared now than I did the first time. For the first twelve months of Poppy's life, I was convinced she would be an only child. *You've done it to yourself, kiddo*, I would think. *There's no way I can do that again.* But now I think the saying is very true: time heals all wounds. And time has given me enough perspective to know that it won't happen again, at least not the same way.

There's every chance my next kid won't sleep either, or that they will have some other issue that makes life very hard. But I know now that being a mother doesn't mean I have to be perfect. All I can do is try my best, be kind to myself, be honest and, most importantly, ask for help when I need it.

2012

ALICE: 'Have I gone mad?'
MAD HATTER: 'I'm afraid so. You're entirely
bonkers. But I will tell you a secret,
all of the best people are.'

—*Alice in Wonderland*

Luke and I were so happy to be back in Brisbane. My family
was there, my close friends were there. I felt so much less
alone and so comfortable. Even though Sydney had been
technically home for Luke, he loved Brisbane's pace and
lifestyle. It was much easier to see ourselves putting down
roots and raising kids in that city, and ultimately that's
what we wanted. We wanted to build our team, a little
squad of Tricketts, who loved the outdoors and exercise,
and just living a peaceful life. We wanted a home and a

happy family. But before that, there was my unfinished business in the pool.

At 27, my body didn't respond or recover as well as it did when I was twenty. I realise it doesn't sound like much of a difference, but it is truly different at the elite level of swimming. This was my greatest challenge, leading into the London Olympics. Mentally, I was a stronger competitor than I had ever been, but my body had lost the advantages of youth. That's just how it was, and I had to deal with it.

Stephan was coming to the end of his coaching career, but he still ran a very professional squad. In some ways, I missed the punishing standards he had once demanded of me, but I didn't know if I could even have met those standards now. I was working incredibly hard just to get back into shape. I didn't shed every single pound that I had gained in my year of inactivity, but I came very close, and the composition of my muscle and skin tone was where it needed to be. I finished 2011 as fit and lean as any elite swimmer should be. Despite everything, despite missing the World Championships and failing to shine at the World Cup, I was still confident that I would make it to London and swim the individual races. All I wanted was one more chance to win gold in the 100-metre freestyle, the race that had always eluded me.

The Olympic trials were held in March 2012 at the South Australian Leisure and Aquatic Centre, in Adelaide. Jess Schipper was there, of course, along with Leisel Jones, Alice

Mills, Stephanie Rice and the Campbell sisters. I was happy to see some familiar faces in the ranks, but there were so many young swimmers I didn't recognise. My generation was thinning out—the boys as well as the girls. It was clearly our last hurrah. We'd travelled very similar roads but the relationships at that meet were unchanged. There was a deep well of respect, but the competition came first. We were all racing for the same precious spots. If anything, we had more at stake, because we knew this was our last chance.

Amongst the ranks of new swimmers were Yolane Kukla and Brittany Elmslie, and Melanie Schlanger who had been around for years but was just hitting her stride was there too, all from Queensland, and all sprinters. They were my new competitors in the freestyle races, and they were incredibly fast. The Campbell sisters were just hitting their peak, dominating the freestyle sprint field. And all of them were significantly younger than me, and hadn't had the time out of the pool. They had completely different body shapes to me, something that I felt had only become more pronounced over the years. My competitors seemed to get taller and taller, with big hands and long limbs that just powered through the water.

I didn't feel threatened, though. In fact, in a way I felt like I had come home. My mind was calm and focused on the task at hand, honed after more than a decade into a tool that was optimised for competition. I didn't think about the changing of the guard. I didn't think about my age. I didn't even think about the coming Olympic Games, because you can't. You can't allow any of those doubts or complications to creep in, because they will sink you. You can't consider the fact that you have a single 53-second window, every four years, in which you can achieve your lifelong ambition, and you may only really be ready for that opportunity once or twice in your career. That is the reality. But reality has no place in dreams. To be the best, you have to still your mind and focus. You have to let go. *I'm strong, I'm fit, I'm healthy, therefore I'm fast. No doubts, no regrets, I'm just here to have fun.*

The first two days of competition were dedicated to the 100-metre butterfly. I came third behind Jess Schipper and Alicia Coutts, trailing by a second, so I missed out on an individual spot at the Olympics. I hadn't regained my peak condition in the butterfly, but I was still disappointed, mostly because qualifying would have taken the pressure off for the rest of the meet. Still, I swam my fastest time in the butterfly since coming out of retirement, and that at least was comforting. My body was excelling under pressure. I realised, though, that it may have been my easiest race because the lactic acid and muscle tiredness hadn't kicked in yet.

The 100-metre freestyle races came on days five and six of trials, and I did what I had to do in the heats and the semis to make it through to the final. In the heats, I swam 35 metres at my full competition pace. I swam 50 metres of the semi-final at full clip, saving my energy for the race that counted. The following day, I stepped up to the block for the finals feeling like I had done everything I could to prepare for this moment.

I went out strong. I didn't spin my wheels when I hit the water and my front-end speed was great, and even coming off the wall I felt like I had form. But in the last 15 metres I felt it ebbing away. Usually, in the last 15 metres, I could reach inside me and draw on an extra reserve of energy to either power myself forward or hold my competitors at bay. But that day in Adelaide, I reached in and there was nothing there. I was at my limit. I swam my best race on the day but it just wasn't fast enough, and I finished fifth in the race.

My reaction was mixed. I knew it was likely I would be selected for the freestyle relay team—the top four were guaranteed; fifth and sixth were discretionary, but were usually selected as backups in case one of the lead swimmers was out of form or got injured. I had never been prouder in my life to qualify for the Olympic Games, because I knew I had truly climbed a mountain, to come out of retirement in very bad shape and make it back onto the world stage. It had been so incredibly hard to get back to that level, and I'd definitely earned my place. But I was incredibly disappointed not to win a spot in the individual 100-metre freestyle event. I wouldn't get the opportunity to race at that top level again, which was something I loved so much. It was my truest, deepest passion, and had driven me for so many years of my life. Now it had slipped from my grasp, and there was nothing I could do about it.

I cried a flood, but they were mostly happy tears. To have set my mind on this Olympic goal and have achieved it was a beautiful thing, and I was old enough and wise enough then to be grateful. I stepped up for the 50-metre freestyle race with a lighter heart. In 24 seconds, it would all be over, one way or another. It wouldn't hurt the way that other races did. I placed fourth behind the Campbell sisters and Yolane Kukla—again, I just didn't have quite enough in the tank. Perhaps I hadn't had enough training time, or enough race experience since my comeback, or maybe it was just that my body was older. So my London Olympics wouldn't involve an individual race—that was that. But I was going to the Olympics for a third time, and that was something truly special.

I had four months from March to July to try to make the cut for the freestyle relay team. That was the last and only goal I had, and my focus sharpened on it like a laser beam. Ten pool sessions a week, cardio, weights, core sessions, bike sessions, always pushing myself to be as fast and as strong as possible. I wasn't swimming butterfly but I continued to do it in training, because the intensity of the stroke improved my cardiovascular fitness and power through the water.

The assumption was always that the top two swimmers would race in the finals at the Olympics, but the third and fourth spots were generally open to selection, based on performances in the heats in London. All the swimmers who were vying for the second two spots would get a run, so I knew I had a chance to prove myself and be in the race for a medal. Many of my competitors were keeping logbooks in training to track their times, repetitions and performances, but I didn't take much notice of that. It could be a source of confidence if you were constantly improving, but I knew it could also be a real downer if for some reason your performance dipped. And what could you really do with that information? I didn't think it would help me. I did the best I could in every training session and I had faith in the process.

Stephan wrote everything down, of course, but he used the information judiciously. If I did a faster time, he told me, otherwise I didn't hear about it. I didn't have to carry the burden of knowing how I fluctuated from day to day. I was free to feel like I was swimming as well at 27 as I had when I was twenty, whether or not that was actually true, and it did wonders for my confidence. I worked, I had faith, I felt emotionally and psychologically free, and that made me as strong as I could be.

Luke and I were strong as well, as strong as we had ever been. Through our time apart, we had learned to really communicate with each other—to talk to each other instead of at each other. We had also learned to work together to do better if something wasn't working for either of us. It was the foundation from which I launched into my dreams and goals, including my final Olympic Games.

London was like a home away from home. The culture seemed not that far removed from ours, and there were so many Australians there when we arrived that it felt like we were playing to a home crowd. It was also the first Games I had attended in an English-speaking country, so everything seemed familiar and I felt comfortable and very supported. I couldn't have asked for anything more. My only concern was whether I would be selected to race, and that decision was entirely in the hands of the coaches. I knew what my capabilities were, and that my body was capable of one great performance, but I was in a position where I had to swim for my life in the heat. I didn't know if I had two top-level swims in me, in one day. The seven hours between the two races wouldn't be enough time for me to recover.

Ahead of the Games, Shannon had told me I was virtually guaranteed a spot in the final team—I assumed this was because of my experience racing at the top level. But by the time we arrived he had revised his position, and I would be swimming for my spot in the heat. I had been trying to be very open and honest with the coaches, and I told them that I couldn't in good conscience swim my top speed just to make the final relay team, knowing that it would be to the detriment of my performance that night. 'I'm going to do the work I need to do to put our team in a good position in the final,' I said. 'But I'll back off if I can, so that I'm capable of racing my best in the final.'

The coaches seemed to accept this, not insisting that I race my fastest, and I did my part to get the team into the final. In the end, however, I wasn't selected. Alicia Coutts, who had placed sixth after me at the Olympic trials and didn't race in the Olympic heats at all, was given the spot for the final race. I felt the fact that she trained at the Australian Institute of Sport may have been a factor, but perhaps that was just my own cynicism. Brit Elmslie took the second discretionary spot because she swam a millisecond or two faster than me in the heat, even though it was clear I had backed off in the final metres. For me, the most devastating thing was that the coaches delivered the news immediately after the heat, as if the selection had been long decided. It all felt so ill-considered.

It was a brutal experience for me, in the midst of an Olympics in which the whole Australian team was struggling. Our swimmers were failing to deliver, and throughout those Games the media scrutiny became more and more intense. It was like failure had given the media an excuse to pull back the curtain on the sport and judge whatever they saw beneath. Leisel Jones was fat-shamed on the front page of a newspaper, which was horrific. Cate Campbell got incredibly sick. Stephanie Rice couldn't live up to her previous phenomenal record and was somehow made to feel small, despite her ongoing issues with a shoulder injury.

James Magnussen, who had an actual advertising campaign declaring that he was going to win an Olympic gold medal, seemed unrecognisable in the water, as if he had collapsed under the pressure; it later emerged that the boys who swam in the men's relay had been having Stilnox parties the week before the Games, which led to an absolute media circus, including an incredibly uncomfortable press conference involving the entire relay team.

I didn't escape the mud-slinging. It was reported that I had an expletive-laden rant in the cool-down area when they told me I hadn't been selected, hurling c-bombs at Shannon and the head coach, Leigh Nugent. This literally did not happen, unless I somehow blacked out and wiped it from my memory. I didn't use the 'c' word at all until many years later, after I started working in radio (and even then I could count the times I've used that word on one hand). But I missed the opportunity to defend myself because I didn't check my voicemail, where a journalist had left a message asking me to respond to the accusations.

After the article came out, I called the journalist and asked him who his source was. 'This is just not who I am, or who I pride myself on being as an athlete,' I told him. 'If someone actually thinks this happened, I need to talk to them about it. It's just not good for the Australian swim team to have toxic stories like this floating around.'

He refused to tell me where he got the story from, which I found incredibly difficult. As disappointed as I was, I really believed I had tried to be a good sport. I know I cried about it when Brit and Alicia were selected, but I tried to keep my hurt private. I was a proud Australian, cheering for my teammates when they won gold in the relay—the only gold medal the Australian swimmers brought home that year.

They had won, so obviously the coaches made the right decision. A very small part of me almost wished that they had come second, though, so I could somehow justify the feeling I had that they would have been better off with me in the team. I was shocked at the decision, and then sad—and then, when I was safely alone with Luke, angry at the politics and subjectivity that I felt had played a role in the decision. Most of all I just wanted to race. It hurt seeing my dream go up in flames.

I had the same passion for swimming in London that I'd had as a little girl, when I'd insisted that Mum let me race with a broken arm. That feverish joy was still there inside me, but I couldn't share it with the world anymore. The feeling was curiously bittersweet, because I finally appreciated how lucky I'd been ever to have had the chance.

London was the end of my swimming career, but it was also the beginning of something very special. As I began to wind down, to stop fixating on the next goal, I was able to look back and start to appreciate all the incredible things I had achieved. Instead of cursing myself and criticising myself and feeling like a failure, I reflected and realised how incredible my career had been. It hadn't come easily. I had worked hard for everything I'd achieved, but I could see how graceful the arc of my career had been, relative to that of other swimmers.

Even the slow, downward swing of that arc was something I could be proud of. I had made it to a third Olympic Games, which was a rare achievement. And because I swam in the heats for the relay team, I took home a gold medal too. It's the one that I most like to share with people, because it was the hardest one for me to earn. The athlete's part of my brain still tells me I didn't actually earn it because I didn't swim in the final, but a far greater part of my brain recognises its true value. It's an imperfect medal, and so it serves as an amazing metaphor for my entire career. It was hard to win, things didn't always go according to plan, and I didn't always execute my role exactly as I intended, but wonderful things still came of it.

It's the medal that best represents me and the career I have been blessed to have. I call it my people's medal, because it represents the whole network of people who supported me. It's one for me, looking back on my achievements with wonder, and for everyone in my life who helped me to live my dreams.

Epilogue

2019

'I never said it would be easy, I only said
it would be worth it.'

—Mae West

No one is what they seem on the surface. Life is long and complicated, full of ups and downs, and it's almost impossible to understand what someone else is going through at any given time. If there is a point to all this, it's that things don't always feel as great as they look, and sometimes they don't look as great as they feel, and it's hard to know the difference unless you listen to someone's story. It's hard to have real empathy for someone unless you're paying attention.

For me, the most interesting stories we can share about ourselves are the ones that are hidden from sight. For most people, I will only ever be Olympic swimmer Libby Trickett, who had a good run in the 2000s. But I'm not just a swimmer. I am not defined by a few gold medals. I'm a wife, a sister, a media personality, an Instagram addict, a daughter and a mum. I'm a dreamer and a ballroom dancing enthusiast. Sometimes I'm on top of the world and sometimes I'm hopeless, just like everybody else. But people don't always see both sides of the coin. The dark side doesn't always make headlines.

My story is as much about struggle and self-doubt as it is about success, and I think it's the struggle and self-doubt that make me human. I've learned to see all the messy, vulnerable parts of my life as the foundation of my perspective and wisdom, so in a way I'm grateful for everything that's happened to me, the bad stuff as well as the good. It has all taught me something.

As a swimmer, I learned the importance of focus and setting goals, and the value of hard work—but as I look back on that period of my life, I know that the real lesson I needed to learn was how to be in the moment, emotionally, and appreciate the wins when they came. I needed to learn how to be kind to myself and forgive myself for making mistakes. I needed to learn that not being perfect is perfectly okay.

As a wife, I have learned how important it is to communicate. I was lucky to meet my soulmate at such a young age, but I never want to take that relationship for granted. As much as Luke drives me bonkers sometimes with his ridiculously rational brain, I know that I am blessed to have him on my team. And to be a good team, we have to be working towards the same goals. We have to check in with each other, talk to each other, make compromises and commitments, every day. I've learned that having fun with your partner is essential too. Otherwise, what are we here for?

In my life after swimming, I've learned that not everything comes easily to me, and that's okay. It's alright to be lost sometimes on the path to finding yourself. It's not even about being good at things, or living up to other people's expectations of you, it's about finding your passion—that thing that pulls you forward like a magnetic force, so that you don't have to push. My whole swimming career was like that, driven by a deep love of the water, and of competition. I was so afraid that I would never feel that passion again, but every step I have taken since I retired for good has been a process of discovery, and I feel like I'm heading in the right direction. I can feel that energy still burning inside of me, and every day I feel more confident that I will find the right outlet for it.

My experiences since I retired have opened up a whole new way of thinking about my body and what it is capable of, because I know now that it's not just a machine that can be trained to compete; it's also an outlet for grief and an inspirer of joy. My body is a wonderful tool that is directly connected to my emotional world, and through it

I have the power to make my life better. That knowledge is something I'd like to share with the world one day, in some new outlet.

Meanwhile, my experiences with mental illness have taught me that it's okay to not be okay. I didn't recognise that I struggled with mental-health issues during my swimming career, and that made so many things so much harder than they needed to be. Like so many people, I subconsciously resisted the idea that there was something 'wrong' with me. Having anxiety or depression was a *weakness*, and I wasn't weak. I just felt really, really awful sometimes, and told myself that was normal. After Poppy was born, when my depression was so intense that it broke through that wall of denial, I learned that real strength comes from reaching out and asking for help when you're down. You're not trapped, you're not alone and there's nothing wrong with you because you're struggling. You're just a human being. We all struggle sometimes. It's okay. If we can all get better at talking about mental health, I think more people will ask for the help they need. I hope more than anything, if you have read my story and you are struggling, that you understand there is hope.

My recovery from postnatal depression has been slow but steady. You don't get better overnight, and there is always a risk that depression and anxiety will return. Sometimes I feel more vulnerable than at other times, and I still have moments of self-doubt, but watching Poppy grow into a lovely, kind little girl has really steadied my heart. When

I saw the goodness in her, I realised that I wasn't a shit parent, and that I hadn't broken my child—she was actually very happy—and that gave me a deep sense of satisfaction and a sense that I was on the right path. When my second daughter, Edwina, was born, we had to navigate a whole new set of issues—severe allergies when she was a newborn, complete with terrible rashes and rivers of diarrhoea—but I felt so much stronger and more capable the second time around. I was certain that I could cope. And if I couldn't cope, I knew there was a safety net.

There probably aren't any gold medals in my future (never say never!), but I don't doubt that there are many glorious moments ahead. Every Saturday morning, I take my girls to the pool and watch them splash around, falling in love with the water just like I did when I was their age, and I am so grateful that I have them in my life. It was all worth it, every dark moment, for the gift that is these two beautiful creatures. They drive me nuts, they have tantrums, they're unreasonable, they demand so much of my attention, but they are totally, absolutely, unbelievably worth it. They have made me a better person.

Today, I am calmer and more confident than I have ever been. Life experiences have given me greater clarity. I know now that swimming, as much as I loved it and continue to love it, is just a sport. It's a game and it should be fun. When a game causes anxiety or grief or pummelling self-doubt, it's a problem.

Funnily enough, I think that if I could go back and have my time in the pool again with what I know now, I'd be a better swimmer, because I'm far more capable of letting go than I ever was as a younger person. After everything I've been through, I feel like I know myself that much more, and I appreciate everything that much more. And no matter what life brings, I know it will be okay in the end.

Acknowledgements

To Luke, thank you for choosing me to share this crazy adventure of life. You have constantly encouraged and enabled me to be better, allowed me to be vulnerable and helped me to chase my dreams. I will be forever grateful for who you are, for our ridiculous sense of humour and the love you surround me with.

To Poppy, Edwina and Baby 3.0 (due in November 2019), being your mother is my proudest achievement. Nothing else will come close. You have all made me a better person and have helped to chart my course in everything that I will do in the future. You fill my heart with a love I never knew could exist. Thank you.

To my mum, your kindness and generosity has known no boundaries and I will always be thankful that I have had your love and guidance.

To Teen, Tootie and Stewy, thank you for being my first friends, helping to shape the person I have become. Things haven't always been easy but you mean so much to me and I could not imagine my life without you in it.

To Stephan, you have been such an important role model in my life. Thank you for being the first person outside of my mum to believe in me. Thank you for teaching me to believe in myself and showing me what I was capable of. I owe so much of where I am today to you.

To my friends and extended family—Jess, Casey, Leith, Kate, Alice, Gregor, Lucas, Tia, Georgie, Ben, Rikki, Sam, Mitch, Kel, Clara and Nick. You guys are my chosen family and I'm the luckiest girl in the world. Thank you for the laughs and the love. I literally couldn't ask for better people in my life.

To Simone, thank you for giving me a voice. Thank you for understanding me and what I wanted to achieve with telling my story. What an incredible gift you have; you are such a wonderful writer and I can't wait to see what you do next.

To the team at Allen & Unwin, I still can't believe that I got to have this amazing opportunity to tell my story and share my experiences. Thank you, Claire, for believing in me from the very beginning. Thank you, Tom and Tom, for supporting me every step of the way. What a wonderful group—I am so grateful that I got to share this little journey with the entire team!

To everyone who supported me during my swimming career, to everyone who stayed up late or woke up early to watch me swim, I don't know if I could ever truly explain what that means to me—then and now. It's hard to comprehend that a complete stranger would do that for you, but it's a love I have had the privilege of feeling, so from the bottom of my heart, thank you.